ACKNOWLEDGMENTS

There are several people who believed in me way before I believed in myself—my husband, Joan Arnold, and Liz Bonham. Other people came along when I was further into my journey and became special to me in ways that only time could show me.

God sent these people to me at critical times in my life when there were two roads to take. Each person has given me the courage, in one way or another, to choose the road that heals. I thank God constantly for their support and love. It would be very difficult to walk alone, but I haven't had to because of the grace that God has extended to me.

To my husband, Keith—Both of our children and I have been greatly blessed because of you. Thank you for supporting me and allowing me to share my story. I love you.

Joan—You are my sister and my best friend. You inspire me and continue to propel me forward as I strive to reach my goals. I believe your encouragement is the reason I am pursuing public speaking. You gave me a vision for my life and believed that I would accomplish whatever I put my mind to. I want to be an inspiration and encouragement to you as well. I will make it a priority to walk beside you and support you all the days of my life. Proverbs 18:24.

Liz—You are a true friend, a loving sister, and an inspiration to me. Over the years I have watched you stay faithful to what you believe in. It is an honor to be your friend. Thank you for painting the cover of this book. What a blessing you are to me!

To all my sisters in Bible study—You have sat patiently around my dining room table and listened to my stories, laughed at my jokes, but most of all supported me in prayer. I consider you my family and cherish each and every one of you. I hope I give out the love to you that you have given to me.

To my therapist—When I think of how my life has changed so dramatically in the last six years I can't help but thank God for you and your ministry. You not only talked about grace while counseling me but showed grace by loving and believing in me. You never gave up on me and always had faith in where my abilities would take me. Because of your wise counsel, I am able to go forward in life and give out to others the truth you showed me. Thank you from the bottom of my heart. Proverbs 4:7.

JoHannah Reardon—Thank you for working with me on this project. I appreciate your time and dedication while helping me write this book. I pray continued blessings over your future in writing, and may peace be with you on your journey.

Out
of
Chaos

A Journey Toward Peace

Penny Arnold

WINEPRESS WP PUBLISHING

Printed in the United States of America.

Packaged by WinePress Publishing, PO Box 428, Enumclaw, WA 98022. The views expressed or implied in this work do not necessarily reflect those of WinePress Publishing. Ultimate design, content, and editorial accuracy of this work are the responsibilities of the author.

Unless otherwise noted, all scriptures are taken from the Holy Bible, New International Version, Copyright © 1973, 1978, 1984 by the International Bible Society. Used by permission of Zondervan Publishing House. The "NIV" and "New International Version" trademarks are registered in the United States Patent and Trademark Office by International Bible Society.

ISBN 1-57921-339-1
Library of Congress Catalog Card Number: 00-110207

CONTENTS

CONTENTS

INTRODUCTION

First, I realized I was living in chaos. Secondly, I realized that there were people out there living lives peacefully. I wanted peace in my life, and I was determined to find it.

To get from chaos to peace was quite a journey. Before I could get out of chaos, I had to face it, define its hold over me, and leave it.

I was in chaos because I was born into it. My family had great wealth, but lived in chaos. It became obvious to me that wealth did not bring peace. My family's chaos exhibited symptoms of manic-depression, disorganized schizophrenia and alcoholism. I had to face that and get free from the power that chaos had over me.

My journey began to follow the steps as described by Scott Peck in *Further Along the Road Less Traveled.*

1. Chaos (life circumstances out of control)
2. Rules (order brought to the chaos)
3. Ambiguity (able to break the rules to act in love)
4. Peace (Value human life more than the rules)

I had to be rigid to leave my chaos and get to order. I had to set clear boundaries so I could see where Chaos ended and Order began. But Order was not Peace. I had to go further. I had to question all of the rules I had accepted in my past and in my present. Black and White reasoning did not work in a gray world, in a grace world. Ambiguity was not a comfortable destination. I knew there was still more road to be traveled. Finally, I found comfort: I moved to Peace.

If you are living in Chaos, I hope my story will inspire you to travel to Peace. I am hoping my story can be a bridge for you to leave your chaos to find your Peace. That is why I have written this book. My life has been changed, and I believe yours can be, too, if you are willing to make the journey.

*The names in this story have been changed to protect those involved.

CHAOS

"Any condition or place of total disorder or
confusion. Obsolete, a vast abyss or chasm."
—WEBSTERS DICTIONARY

1

MEET MY FAMILY

My smile felt glued to my face as my jaws began to ache. I was afraid that my grin was beginning to look like a grimace. I looked down to smooth my Ralph Lauren skirt, purchased especially for the occasion. At least looking down I could give my facial muscles a rest.

When I lifted my head, the sea of faces in the audience began to come into focus. I recognized fellow students and professors here at the university I attended looking toward the man at the microphone as he continued his introduction.

"I am pleased to introduce the one who made this fine facility we are now meeting in possible. Most of you know who he is by his very successful chain of discount stores, which many of us visit regularly. No other individual has ever given this university such a large donation. One thing I admire about this man is his attitude toward and his devotion to the church. Let's give him a warm welcome of thanks."

Everyone rose applauding enthusiastically as my grandfather ascended to the stage. As I stood up with the crowd, I gloried in the attention of my peers at this large Christian university. When the crowd finally settled down, my grandfather's deep, raspy voice filled the auditorium.

"Thank you for that kind reception. And thank you for what you are doing here. I believe our Christian colleges have been doing a fine job educating our young people. These are the ones who are going out to teach the gospel to the world.

"My family and I have no use for a religion that doesn't affect a person's daily life. We begin and end each day in prayer, thanking God for all He's done for us. We never miss church unless we're ill. The old saying is, 'If you believe in something, you'll put your money where your mouth is.' That is exactly what we are doing today."

The applause again crescendoed as he gave the president of the university a warm hug and made his way off the stage.

My smile felt truly painful now and I couldn't help rubbing my face to give it relief, but I would keep smiling. After all, I wanted everyone to see me as I was. I wanted them to realize what a deeply religious, wealthy family I came from. They must see that I had it all.

"What were you thinking about! I'm not going to let you get away with that!"

I huddled down in my room and tried to continue coloring the picture I was working on but my crayon froze in mid-air when I heard my brother being thrown against the wall. At least I wasn't in trouble this time. If Daddy couldn't figure out who did something, he lined us all up to get whacked with the belt. But Mike always got it the worst. The sounds coming from the other side of the house made my stomach churn and set my mind racing. My fear was rising within like a monster working his way out of a deep pit as I thought about that certain look daddy got when his anger built up. Anything would set him off and so I kept expecting him to come into my room next. Running into my mom's room I cried,

"Mommy, stop Daddy from hitting Mike!" She didn't respond. She just continued to sit on the bed and stare into the television set.

"Mommy, get Daddy to stop!" It's as if she didn't hear me. She just kept watching *The Dick Van Dyke Show*. Completely ignoring the dramatic scene going on in the house, Mom finally said something.

"I love those pants that Mary Tyler Moore is wearing."
Mom already decided to give up.

One of the ways Mom learned to cope with her pain was by going shopping. She went shopping every day and it became her favorite form of entertainment. I remember the day my mom went to buy me shoes.

Entering the shoe aisle, I saw some really cool shoes. "Mama, look at these. I want them!"

"No, Penny, you don't like those. You like the black softies over here."

She led me to the same shoes I had worn for as long as I could remember and we traded my old pair for a new identical pair. I never got a chance to form my own opinion so I concluded, "I don't really like shoes," and began to go barefoot at every opportunity.

I never got a chance to grow my hair out either and was somehow convinced I needed to keep it short. "Couldn't I let my hair grow, Mama? Life would be perfect if I could fix my hair in pig tails."

"Nonsense, Penny! You are so cute in that little pixie cut. It's perfect for you and it makes your eyes look so big."

My peers never did mention my eyes being big but they did make fun of me constantly for looking like a boy. I tried to use looking like a boy to my advantage a few times, however; I ended up in trouble for it when I was in third grade and never did it again.

I decided to go to the recreation center one hot summer day and when I got there I noticed a bunch of boys playing basketball. I wanted to play so I joined in. I told them my name was Mike and I joined the fun. I was pretty good at sports so I fit in just great until someone decided we needed to split up into teams.

"Skins and shirts guys! Mike you're skins."

This boy continued telling everyone who was what and I just stood there frozen. I knew that skins was the team without shirts.

"Well Mike, are you gonna play or just sit there?"

I darted out of there so fast they barely saw me leave. I never pretended to be a boy again.

I really never knew who I was as a kid. I let other people define me, and what my schoolmates thought of me was no exception.

School! Just the word made me start to get nervous. School and I just didn't seem to get along—too many rules or something. I was too loud and got into endless fights. School started with our participation in a new car-pool. I could at least fit in for a few minutes as I drove to school with all the other kids until the day it was my mom's turn to pick us up.

"Where's your Mom, Penny? Almost all the other kids are gone. I've gotta get home for piano lessons."

I shrugged my shoulders. "She'll be here in a minute." I looked hopefully down the street, expecting our shiny Cadillac at any moment.

After another ten minutes, Bobby said, "I'm calling my mom. I'm tired of waiting." Slowly, all of my carpool friends drifted in to call their parents. As they drove off one by one, I continued to wait expectantly, finally resigning myself to the long walk home. When I got home, Mom was sitting on the bed watching television.

A few days later, I sat on the step of our beautiful home waiting for my ride. I was so proud of our sprawling ranch style house with its arched windows and gabled roof. The winding driveway went all the way around the house past a turreted room to the back where there was a very large yard. I knew even at my young age that this was a very good neighborhood. After all, many of the Dallas Cowboys lived here, which I heard my parents tell many a visitor to our home.

It finally dawned on me that I had been sitting here a long time. I walked slowly up the steps into the house.

"Mama, my ride never came."

Mama began to laugh. "Do you know what? I just got a phone call. It was my turn to drive." She continued to giggle nervously. "Oh well. I guess we won't be part of that silly ol' carpool after all. You can just ride your bike."

So much for the carpool kids. I ended up riding my bike to school with my best friend. I enjoyed riding my bike so I always wondered why I had to go through the whole carpool mess to begin with.

2

CHURCH

I liked going to church because I felt I truly belonged there. School meant trouble for me, but church and I got along. There were lots of fun moments and good friends, who I felt accepted me for who I was. I must admit that I didn't understand most of what went on in the service, however. As a very young child, I got warts all the time and I remember singing my favorite song *Holy, Holy, Holy* that had a line "Which, wert, and art, and evermore shalt be." I thought the song said, "Who, warts and all and evermore shall be." I loved that because I thought that meant that God had warts just like me!

After we sang, they would pass around grape juice and crackers for communion and after communion they would circulate the collection plate. My brother told me that communion was snack time and then you had to pay for it.

The church backed up to a big, open field. After church we would all feed the horses, then roll down the big grassy hill on the side of the church building. Daddy brought two bags of candy to church every Sunday and gave it to Mr. Bruce, better known as the Candy Man. He'd pass out candy corn and peppermints to all the kids after church.

My Sunday School teacher, Mrs. Linda, made the Bible come alive. I will always remember her story about Moses and the plagues of Egypt. Each week she talked about a different plague. I remember thinking, "Why won't that mean king let those people out of prison?" The last plague was really scary.

"Children, this king was so stubborn, that finally God told him that unless he let the people go, He would have to kill the oldest son in each family, including the king's own boy. Well, that king still wouldn't listen, so God had to do it. Finally, the king let the people go. Imagine who it would have been in your family and how awful that would be."

All the way home I stared at Mike. Boy, was I glad that I wasn't him!

Because I enjoyed church, I couldn't see the hypocrisy that was rampant. Most confusing was my family's apparent devotion to their religion.

I believe my family was doing the best they could with what they had to work with. Everyone was trying hard to make life work and a big part of trying to "do it right" was going to church and looking spiritual. It made everyone feel justified about who they were because at least they were "doing" something constructive to cover up the problems.

I have to go back to my family roots to examine where some of the problems started.

My grandfather walked out on my grandmother when my mom was three years old. He had an affair with his secretary and ran off with her when she found out she was pregnant. Most people didn't know about my grandmother and thought my grandfather's second wife was my biological grandmother. People would tell me all the time that I looked just like my grandmother and I always wanted to say, "Which one?"

My grandfather never did take responsibility for walking out on his wife and daughter. His way of showing love and remorse was by sending them money or things. Over time, I believe my grandfather learned a pattern that seemed to work for him.

Because of his ability to make enormous amounts of money, he would cover up his pain and guilt by giving away huge donations, making sure his name was on each one. The attention and approval my grandfather received from the generous gifts were enough for him to feel okay about his life. It became easier and easier to justify his actions because over time his conscience was seared. The mind can do incredible things to protect a person from dealing with their hurt and pain.

The message I received loud and clear was that "God's grace is measured by how much he has bestowed upon a person." I grew up seeing church and donations being used to define one's spiritual walk. A person's righteousness was demonstrated by how much money he gave away or how much he went to church. Money and power can corrupt good people because it is so easy to measure yourself by what the public sees in you and not ask God what he sees in you.

In order to fit in with people who possess wealth and power, one must try to conform to some extent. It is very hard to stay balanced when you are constantly being thrown into this type of lifestyle. When a person has the money to wine and dine themselves, it is almost impossible to be able to relate to "the other side of the tracks." Donations can make a person feel as if he has gone over to the other side and become part of the solution when, in fact, it only causes a bigger problem for the giver to deal with later if his/her motives are to try and feel better about him/herself.

Just as money donations were used to create an illusion of spirituality, going to church was too. When we were on vacation it was unacceptable to miss church on Sunday so no matter where we were, Dad would find a place to worship. If he couldn't find a church within our denomination, we would end up in a graveyard somewhere and stand around some strange person's headstone and do church. As a little girl I felt the hypocrisy and it created a very strange feeling inside of me. I hated that feeling and wanted out of there so badly. It was all about rules and control rather than love and grace. Somehow it was important that we all looked good on the outside.

3

GROWING UP IS HARD TO DO

When I was a small child, my dad was involved with the family business and owned three of the retail outlet stores in Colorado. Four times a year my grandfather would rent out the whole Dallas Market Center so that buyers from all over the country would order merchandise for their franchises. Mom and Dad would fly to Dallas for the shows and hire a babysitter to stay with us for the week.

My favorite was Mrs. Hollingsworth who made popcorn balls and colored with me on the couch. Once we had a mean lady by the name of Mrs. Olsting who got mad at my sister and pushed her down the stairs. When my daddy said he fired her, in my young mind I imagined that he put her in a field and set her on fire.

It always made me happy when they took us with them to Dallas. "Let's get ready kids. Make sure you've got everything packed. The plane is leaving in an hour."

We would all frantically get everything ready to go. As children we were responsible for organizing ourselves even when we were young.

"This show is going to be special. Cary Grant is going to be there to help promote the stores. We'll make our entrance in Granddaddy's private helicopter."

I didn't know who Cary Grant was but everyone seemed to think it was a big deal so their enthusiasm carried over to me. I made sure I threw his name around a lot after that.

"When we get to the show, feel free to pick out any merchandise you want. Granddaddy says you can have whatever suits you."
I hung on Mama's words and couldn't help staring at her. She was dressed in her Neiman Marcus best and even in my tender years I knew she was a knockout. At home I poured over the photos of her at the beauty pageant she won at eighteen. I loved the way strangers turned to stare at her and felt proud that she was my mother. These were the best times for our whole family because everyone got what they wanted in terms of recognition and possessions.

I spent a lot of time with my grandmother growing up. My grandmother was a shrewd businesswoman in her own right and owned one of the family's franchise stores. She took me to work with her but also spent a lot of time with me at her home. We spent hours playing cards in her enclosed porch that overlooked the city. She was always kind to me and would call me her "golden child."

One of the most confusing things at Grandmama's house was the strange girl on the couch. She was very frail and blind, demanding twenty-four hour care. I never quite understood how she fit into our lives since there was an unwritten rule that you didn't talk about her or ask questions unless my parents brought her up in conversation.

I finally worked up the courage to ask my sister about her.

"Patty, how does the girl on the couch fit into our family?"

"She was our sister but Grandmama owns her and that's why she lives with her and not us."

This was the only explanation I got, not understanding until years later that my grandmother had legal custody of my sister. It was as if she never existed in our home. When outward appearances make up the substance of your life, whatever doesn't fit must be excluded. There was no place for a handicapped child in our lives.

Looking back now, I believe my grandmother did not adopt my sister out of love. As sick as it may seem, there were many times my grandmother would use my sister as a tool to inflict more pain on an already difficult situation. There was so much resentment and unresolved anger between my grandmother and mother, and they were never honest with each other about their feelings. Acting nice to each other on the outside was just a cover-up.

Dad would call my grandmother every Sunday and make my mom get on the phone and talk to her. This seemed very thoughtful of my dad even though the conversations were not all that great. However, as I grew older I realized that Dad didn't want their relationship to deteriorate because of all the money at stake.

The way we were perceived by others ruled our lives. One sure sign of things not being quite right could be detected in the animals that we owned. When Mom brought home our cat, Babes, she explained there were a few minor details to work through such as de-clawing and potty training. Mom never did things the typical way. She wanted our cat, Babes, to be one of us so she found a book on how to potty train a cat without using a litter box. This became her project for a while. The book instructed her to buy a baby potty-chair, which my mother promptly did.

"Mom, what are you going to do with that potty chair?" I knew there wasn't a toddler living in our house.

"I'm going to put Babe's cat litter in the bowl!"

"The cat's going to use a potty chair?" I asked with confusion.

"Oh no. Babes is going to learn to go just like the rest of us. Once I teach Babes to jump on the baby potty and use it, I'll take it away and she'll learn to use the big one just like us!"

We already shared our eating dishes with the cat so why not the toilet? It worked to a certain degree so within a few weeks we were sharing the toilet with Babes. She never mastered it very well so now we had to share a bathroom with an eccentric cat and still had to change the litter in the cat box.

My parents loved to entertain and were always on their best behavior in order to impress our guests. Dad shined in this arena because he loved to draw attention to himself. This particular night he chose his red flannel, plaid pants. We never knew who the guests would be because Dad asked whomever he was trying to work a business deal with. At least these strangers had an opportunity to make a memory at our house!

As all the guests were seated at the dining room table, my brother kept leaning back in his chair.

"Mike, keep all four legs of the chair on the ground," Mom told him repeatedly. Halfway through the meal, Mike forgot and once more did his balancing act. We all heard the crash before we saw Mike sitting on the floor with the legs of the chair broken off in all four directions. The crash scared the cat so that she leaped onto the fichus tree in the corner of the room, raised her tail and did her business right there in front of everyone. At least she hit the potting soil below. I still don't know if our cat, Babes, was a product of her environment or if she was born weird!

We moved to Dallas the summer of my fifth grade year. I wanted to fit in with this group of kids so badly but they were more advanced than my friends in Colorado were. Girls were already going steady with boys and some girls were talking about going to "second and third base" with their boyfriends. I quickly learned that first base was kissing, second base was above the waist and third base was below the waist. Of course you can figure out a home run. A girl in my class got pregnant the summer after our sixth grade year and there was talk of an abortion. I can see now that if it weren't for my friends at church, I could easily have made the same mistakes, but somehow I kept my innocence.

A boy approached me one afternoon on the playground and asked me to "go with him." I replied, "Where?" Everyone laughed at me but I didn't know what he meant.

Parties consisted of "spin the bottle" and "truth or dare." We would all sit around a circle and if the bottle pointed in your direction, it was your turn to go in the closet and kiss a certain boy. I ended up with Jeff Beaman and we kissed but I didn't see the thrill in it all. This new environment was unknown territory for me and everything I did seemed to be wrong.

As I was trying to adjust to life at school, I watched Mike and Dad's relationship disintegrate. Things were never good between them, but as Mike grew older the confrontations grew worse. Dad would get angry and begin yelling, "Hit your old man, Son. Let go of your anger and fight like a man!" Mike would stand there silently, frozen in fear. "Come on. Don't you have any guts?" Mike remained immovable without responding. It would make Dad even madder and he would start punching him until he had to fight back.

After one of Mike and Dad's heated exchanges, Mike left for good. He was only fifteen or sixteen years old, but after Dad hit him a few times, ranting and raving, Mike went to his room, packed his stuff and walked out. Dad never knew he left because when the argument was over, he went to his room and took a nap.

We didn't know where Mike went. Eventually we found out that he rented a room with the money he earned at his after-school job. I was too afraid for my own safety to ask any questions. Mike's interaction with the family became sporadic after this.

Patty got it worse than I did, too, probably because she was the oldest. Dad left bruises on her more than once and she would tell her teachers that she fell down the stairs.

By the time I got to junior high, I was very insecure. I had no real friends and hung around with the "nerd" group. I tried out for cheerleading and was so excited when I made it past the judges. The next step was making it past the student body, which was terrifying. I chose to do the "Victory Cheer". Loudly I yelled, "V-I-C-T-O-R-S" and then "C-O-U-G-A-R-Y". I was mortified when I started hearing giggles and snickers, realizing everyone was laughing at me. I ran off the stage in tears. My big chance to be popular, and I blew it!

High school was not much better because I was never known as Penny but as Patty's little sister. Patty was very well liked and knew all the right things to do and say at the perfect time. She won "Senior Favorite" a few years before. I just couldn't catch on and wondered, *How does she do it?*

It seemed all my dates were a disaster. Once when a boy came to pick me up, he asked if he could use the bathroom. I pointed him in the right direction. A minute later I heard a yell and a door slam. "Whoa! Excuse me!"

"What's wrong?" I called out.

"I walked in on your cat. Is there another bathroom I can use?"
It ended up being a short date. Instead of going out to eat and a movie, he said he wasn't hungry, took me to the twilight movie, then back home. I never heard from him again.

4

MONEY, MONEY, MONEY

My father continually had a new money making project because my parents always wanted more money than they had. None of these were successful.

The deep hurt I experienced growing up came from my knowing that Mom and Dad could have given me so much more but they chose the get rich quick schemes over me. I can go back in my mind and recount several different times my parents fell prey to people's moneymaking ideas.

My parents got involved with numerous schemes. The Cambridge diet was a shake that was supposed to take off unwanted pounds without any sacrifice made on the customer's part. This business was set up in a pyramid atmosphere, designed to recruit other people to sell the product while the recruiter shared in the profits of what was sold. Mom bought cases of this powder formula and the only person who made money was the man who sold it to her.

Then there was "Puridyne", also set up in the pyramid format, which was a machine designed to purify the air.

The Medic-Madic machine designed to detect cancer anywhere in the body was another scheme my parents put money toward.

There was the time a man came to my dad and said he needed thousands of dollars to get his electric car on the market. He asked my dad for the money and assured him he would receive a large return on his money investment and as usual, Dad gave it to him.

One would think my parents would have given up on these money making schemes after awhile but they didn't. Mom heard of a man who made money by buying Mercedes overseas and then selling them for a profit here in the states. She went to Europe and bought a couple of these cars and brought them back. She took a huge loss.

My favorite story is Amway. We were instructed not to tell anyone that my dad was involved in this because his way of "roping" people into this business was by asking them over for a casual dinner and then pulling out the chalkboard when they least expected it. If they knew ahead of time, it would ruin the surprise.

He bought thousands of dollars of Amway products so he would receive a special ranking in the system. We lived with these products for years afterwards. My dad even came up with a solution to keep his business secret. Anytime we needed to talk about the subject of Amway, we were to call it "Um um." We actually had conversations where we said "Um um this" and "Um um that." Thinking about it makes me laugh even now.

After losing a great deal of money in the stock market, we moved into an apartment. This wasn't the first time my parents called on my grandfather for help. Our house burned down a few years earlier and my dad didn't have any insurance so my grandfather bought them another house in the same neighborhood. My parents decided to deal with this crisis in their usual manner.

"Betty, let's have your dad over for dinner."

They made sure to let my grandfather know that they had run into some bad luck and it all worked like clockwork.

My grandfather was duly horrified that his daughter was living in an apartment so he promptly bought them a house that he kept in his name. However, this house was not nearly as opulent as the last one. The home we had been living in was definitely upper class. It was a sprawling ranch style with large double doors under a high arched entryway. The four-gabled roof and many paned windows above a courtyard shrieked wealth to those who came to see us. My dad made sure to tell everyone about the large pool we had in the backyard. But this house was middle class since it was smaller and in a more average neighborhood. Besides being more humble, there were obvious flaws such as the crack in the front door and the ivy that had begun to crumble the brick. My parents saw this as a great humiliation. Because social standing meant everything, all meaning and purpose disintegrated from our lives. Everything began to crumble.

In spite of my mother's beauty, she began to look increasingly bizarre. She purchased numerous wigs to cover her unkempt hair and relied on flamboyant clothes and jewelry rather than tasteful ones to portray an illusion of wealth. She also began to drink heavily, adding to her scattered thinking and slovenly appearance.

She completely gave up cleaning the house. The sheets were not changed for months. The white lining on my parent's bedspread turned to brown. You could actually see the clumps of dust on the white iron light fixture that hung over their bed. Thank goodness I had my own bathroom so I could at least control that part of my life. I became obsessive in my own cleaning habits. My father dealt with the dirt and roaches by putting blue roach powder everywhere. It started at the front step and blazed a trail into the house. Every room was outlined in it.

No repairs were made at this house. A friend of mine helped me get some of my things out of our attic. Trying to balance our way through all the clutter, I heard a crash.

"What happened, Brad?"

"My foot went through the ceiling! Help me out."

After struggling to get him out, we both stared at the gaping hole.

"If I hadn't caught myself on that beam, I'd have fallen all the way through. Your parents are going to have a lot to do to fix that."

The playful giggle that had started when I saw Brad fall through the ceiling, now became a roar of laughter. But even I couldn't have guessed that the ceiling would not be fixed for ten years.

My parent's goal was to make more money for their use only, which did not extend to me.

I worked hard to save money as a teenager to buy a car, but I naively gave my paychecks to my parents to cash. On more than one occasion, I didn't get the money. It happened to Mike, Patty and me several times but because of our fear, we didn't question it. I received some stock from my grandfather when I was sixteen.

"Penny, you need to sign this piece of paper for me so I can cash your stock at the bank."

"Sure, Dad." I obediently signed.

After a few days had gone by, I became curious about the money.

"Dad, did you get my stock cashed?"

"It is your obligation as a family member to help out around here. I needed it."

I knew not to question the rules. This greedy attitude of my parents produced other strange quirks. One of them was our family's habit of eating out which was one of our favorite forms of entertainment.

As soon as we were old enough to get a job, we were responsible for purchasing everything with our own money. Mom and Dad would announce that we were going out for dinner. Once there, they would let each of us order whatever we wanted. They waited until last.

"And Sir, what can I get you?"

"Oh, I'm not hungry. Just bring me a cup of coffee."

"What about you, Ma'am?"

"Coffee's fine for me too."

When our meals came, we soon found out why our parents didn't order. They just helped themselves to various items on our plates, which we had to pay for!

My brother found a way around this when he was newly married. When he and his wife, Ann, came home for the holiday, our parents announced that we would go out to breakfast at 8:00 the next morning. Mike set the alarm for 5:30 A.M.

"Ann, get up."

"It's too early. Why did you wake me up?"

"You'll see. Just get dressed and come with me."

She went along with him and they had a full meal early that morning. At 8:00, they were back at the house ready to go out. We all piled in the car and went to Denny's and one by one everyone ordered coffee except Patty and I.

"Aren't you getting anything, Son?"

"No, I'm not hungry."

"You have to eat!"

"No, thank you."

Mike winked at Ann while Patty and I shared our food!

Restaurants with Dad were always interesting. There was the time he got on top of the table and started doing a dance. He's 6'3" and weighs 210 lbs. so this was a notable event! When he had the attention of the whole dining room, he poured a glass of water on his head. What precipitated this event, I don't know. Dad was in his manic state of mind at the time.

At one restaurant, we were waiting to pay for a meal and the line was getting pretty long. Nobody came to check us out so Dad got behind the counter and started working the cash register. When the register popped open, it got the attention of a waitress who immediately went to get the manager. My mom took us out to the car and a few minutes later my dad came out.

He commented, "That manager sure doesn't know how to take a joke."

My sister coined a saying to deal with all the craziness of our household. N.B.D. stood for "No Big Deal", which became our rallying cry.

5

N.B.D.

The experiences we had could supply a sitcom with material for months. Holidays were particularly crazy around our house. Like a lot of families, a big part of Thanksgiving is the turkey. I look back now and feel sorry for "Mr. Gobbles." He already went through so much by the time he got to our house but as always, he wouldn't forget his short stay with us!

Mom had unique ways of dealing with a bird. She might purchase it five or six years in advance with her "buy one get one free" coupon. Somehow it always tasted fine.

Her ritual for cooking a turkey was always the same. She would unwrap him, place him on a platter and put him out on the front porch to thaw in the fresh, warm Texas air. It always seemed to work until one year when the bird "flew" away.

"Where did that turkey go to? I can't find it anywhere. It must have just flown off."

Soon the family was all involved.

"It couldn't have just flown off, Mom. It has to be somewhere."

We searched behind the bushes and all around the porch to find where it could have fallen. Finally Mom spotted it in the neighbor's yard.

"What do you know. The cat drug it off. Look at all the bite marks on it. Oh well, he's a little shaken but not badly injured. I'll just wash him up."

Sure enough, she cleaned him up, cut off the chewed parts and cooked the turkey. It tasted fine to me. To our family this was just N.B.D.

Even worse was the time she made chili. I now find this horrifying but at the time it was N.B.D. Dad started a big pot of chili but then got busy doing something else so Mom took over.

"Where's the big spoon I use to stir with?"

She looked around the kitchen for a few minutes until I saw the light go on in her eyes. After disappearing into the laundry room for a few minutes, she came out with the spoon. I noticed there was gray dirt covering it when it dawned on me.

"Mom! That's not the pooper-scooper spoon you use in the cat box is it?"

Mom just laughed, "Don't tell Dad!"

She continued to stir the chili with this spoon. Nobody died and nobody told until now.

<hr>

The bank got used to my mother, calling her by name with each visit. They couldn't help but notice the zip-lock bag she used to keep all her money in. Every time Mom walked in the bank, she would dump every item of her purse out on the teller's counter to find it for her deposit. All heads turned toward her at the clatter of change hitting the counter and spilling on the floor as she scrambled through the mess in order to find loose change and dollar bills.

There were also a few times that she took the deposit canister from the drive-through. Her account was charged twenty-five dollars for not returning it but she found a good use for each one. She put her jewelry in one container and even stored Babe's cat food in a few!

On a trip to Paris my sister and mother raved about the great shopping, but had a little more trouble with the food. Not only were they eating foreign dishes, but they also had to try to figure out what the menu said in the first place. They entered a quiet little restaurant that smelled wonderful, as odors of fresh bread, spices and cheeses mingled together. Patty kept perusing the French menu for something that looked familiar. Mother, however, knew exactly what she wanted and how to get it. When the waitress arrived, Patty ordered an item she thought she recognized. Not Mom! She tucked her hands under her armpits waving her arms up and down as she did a full-blown imitation of a chicken, complete with squawks. I don't know the waitress's reaction, but my sister laughed so hard that the water she was drinking came out her nose. Evidently the waitress understood because Mom enjoyed her chicken while Patty stared at her unrecognizable foreign dinner.

I can laugh at many of these experiences but some of them cause me to shudder to this day. One in particular was my dad's driving habits. He wrote the book on road rage. He often got mad at someone and cut him off at high speeds. I saw him deliberately hit someone in his car, make it look like his fault and sue him. He would win too! Lawsuits were common in our home.

In high school, our family had something going on across town. Patty and I planned to leave early so we decided to take a separate car. We didn't know the way so we agreed to follow our parents, then back track our way home afterwards.

Heavy rain and fog made it difficult to see. Patty was trying hard to keep up with Dad but he was going at least seventy miles-per-hour. We laughed as we weaved in and out of traffic, making jokes about keeping up with the taillights of Dad's car.

Suddenly Patty quit laughing and said, "Does Daddy have a taillight out?"

"Patty, we're following the wrong car! We've lost him. Stay on the highway and hopefully Dad will realize we're not behind him."

We both began laughing hysterically which was our typical response when we were nervous, but we knew we were in big trouble.

A few minutes later we noticed a car that had pulled over to the side. We stopped behind him as Dad stormed out of his car, slamming the door.

"Penny, you drive! You can do a better job of keeping up than Patty can. What is wrong with you girls?" His thundering voice echoed in my ears as he stomped back to his car.

I looked at Patty in terror. "I can't drive. You have lots more experience than I do. Just keep driving; he'll never know."

"No way. I'm not going to get in trouble again. You move over into this driver's seat and get going."

"If you make me do this, I'll tell Dad about last night when you snuck out with Kathy Smith and her friends."

"You wouldn't!"

"Oh yes, I would!"

Patty drove.

We made it in one piece but got lost on the way home. By the time we made it back, Mom and Dad were in bed asleep. So much for taking two cars!

Many years later, having two cars turned out to be a good thing for me. My aunt died and I decided to go to her funeral. I was eight and a half months pregnant and wasn't in the mood to participate in all the activities going on afterwards, so my sister and I took a separate car.

It was close to one hundred degrees that day and I was over two hundred pounds. We had a forty-five minute drive and my feet were so sweaty that I decided to take off my shoes until we got to the funeral.

"Put your shoes on Penny, we're almost there."

After trying to get my shoes back on I realized they wouldn't go on. "My feet have swollen up Patty and there is no way these shoes are gonna go back on my feet!"

"Keep trying."

"It's no use, I'm gonna have to go barefoot!"

Patty immediately stopped at the first grocery store we could find and we ran down the shoe isle.

"What about these house slippers?" I asked frantically as I was slipping them on my bare feet.

"No way Penny! Put these tennis shoes on."

After trying to squeeze my foot into my normal size seven, I quickly realized that I would need a much larger size to fit my swollen feet and ankles. I finally got to the size ten and it went on.

"Well Patty, they might be a little long but the width will work."

"Just get them; we're already late."

My feet flapped down the isle and we were on our way.

We pulled up to the grave sight and went to sit down. I was sweating profusely trying to figure out why anyone would conduct a funeral service outside in this Texas heat. Halfway through the sermon, the preacher opened up the coffin. I was in shock. My aunt was lying in this coffin with a full-length mink coat and draped with all her diamonds!

I looked at my sister and said, "Man, she's gotta be hot!"

Patty quickly responded, "Do you mean she's hot in that box or hot somewhere else?"

We began to laugh so hard that I couldn't contain myself. I got up to leave and fell over my feet. The preacher stopped the service and everyone started to stare at me because they all thought I was going into labor.

I got up and escaped into my car, took off the clown shoes and drove off, making sure the air conditioner was on full blast! N.B.D.

6

COLLEGE YEARS

I loved going away to college because nobody compared me to my sister and people only knew my family by reputation, not reality.

Getting away made me more aware that something wasn't right at my house. While I was with my family, I was so enmeshed that I couldn't see the dysfunction. However my values were firmly entrenched by this time. I threw my family name around a lot. Everyone knew about my grandfather's stores and how much money he had donated to the university. I often talked about our world travels to Europe, Japan, South America and Hawaii. I wore jewelry obnoxiously to show off the family wealth. It was my weapon to intimidate people, as well as a way to make me feel secure.

Regardless, I knew that my life was not normal. I could see for the first time that other people did not live the way my family did and I began to long to get my life straightened out. Confusion plagued me so I visited a counselor on campus to try to get some advice. When I mentioned a few problems with my parents, this man told me he couldn't help me because his schedule was all booked up. I knew a lot of kids who continued to get help from this man. It wasn't until later that I realized that the huge donations my family gave prevented anyone from looking deeper into our family's issues.

In spite of all this, I liked school and made some genuine friendships. The most significant friendship was with a tall, red-haired young man named Robert. Robert was well liked and ran with a great group of people that I very much wanted to be a part of. His quiet, self-controlled manner appealed to me. He brought balance to my outgoing personality. We hit it off in every way.

Of course, the inevitable day came when I had to introduce him to my parents. I'll let Robert explain his first impressions:

Penny tried to warn me a bit about her parents but nothing prepared me for what I saw when I got to their home. It was impossible to ignore the three-inch trail of blue roach powder that led the way into the house. The inside was an absolute disaster. I'd never seen anything more neglected and wondered if maybe they didn't know I was coming.

We went to an exotic restaurant at Bachman Lake in Dallas. Leopard skins covered the walls and Penny's mother wore her house slippers and drank her Chablis wine. I didn't recognize anything on the menu except frog legs so that's what I ordered. I thought I could get along with anyone but this was a world I'd never experienced before. I got lost when the conversation turned to alligator purses, Rolexes and diamonds.

My overwhelming thought was that if I could just get Penny back to the dorm, I'd never have to see her again! I couldn't imagine being connected with her family. But somehow when we got back to school and it was just Penny and I again, the memory faded. I married her six months later.

My wedding would make Miss Manners pass out. It was a day I'll never forget but not because of any sentimental memories. I didn't have any money for a wedding or a dress and I knew my parents weren't going to offer me any money for help so I found a place that rented wedding dresses for fifty dollars an hour. I actually found a pretty gown and veil that worked.

I got to my wedding and there were no decorations in the auditorium. Mom kept saying that the cherry wood pews and emerald green carpet were so pretty that they didn't need anything extra added to them. I just wanted to get married so I wasn't too concerned with all the details.

My mom was barefoot at the reception and I'm sure had a few Chabli wines by this time. When I walked in the banquet hall I wasn't too surprised to see my wedding cake sitting on a board covered with tin foil. The tablecloth was a green bed sheet spread over a card table. I didn't have to worry about a professional photographer showing up because he didn't.

I remember telling my sister that my wedding dress had to be back to this rental place within the hour because I didn't want to go over the fifty-dollar limit. My grandmother heard me and asked, "What happened to all the money I sent your momma for this wedding?"

My mom of course had pocketed all the money she had sent.

I responded, "Well I don't know but if it's anywhere in the fifty-dollar range, I'll be glad to ask her so I can at least have my dress paid for!" I was serious.

At the wedding, we received numerous gifts. Since we had to be back at school on Monday, I left many of them at my parent's house. When Robert and I came back to pick them up, several were missing. The next door neighbor asked me if I liked the silverware she gave me and I told her that I never received it. My mom overheard the conversation so she ran into the living room to "explain."

"You know, I knew Penny liked a different pattern so we took that one back. We'll go get another one." I knew I'd never get that silverware or the money that Mom kept.

Dad's inappropriate behavior was continually a problem. Robert and I were living in Fort Worth when my dad came over to visit us at our apartment one afternoon. He knocked on the door and I let him in.

"Hi Penny. Is it alright if I use your bathroom?"

"Sure, Dad. It's right down the hall."

After about thirty minutes had gone by, Robert began to ask questions.

"What's he doing in there, Penny? Do you think he's alright?"

"I don't know. Do you suppose I should check on him?"

"Yes!"

I walked to the bathroom door and knocked timidly. "Dad, are you okay in there?"

"Sure. The door's not locked. Come on in."

I cracked the door open only to see my father's clothes on the floor. When I looked up, I found him in the bathtub soaking! I quickly shut the door and made my way back to Robert. I tried to keep my voice light.

"No problem, Robert. He's just taking a bath."

Robert stared at me open-mouthed, slowly shaking his head in astonishment. "Something's not right about that man!"

"Oh Robert, you are so critical of my family!"

Could I have been in denial?

To my knowledge, Robert has never actually eaten at my parent's house. It didn't take him long to figure out that Mom didn't go to Martha Stewart's cooking school.

"Penny, I need a glass of water."

"The glasses are over the sink. Help yourself."

Robert came back a moment later but there was no glass in his hand.

"Penny, come here," he whispered.

"What is it?"

He led me to the sink where Mom had left the turkey baster resting on the side of the platter. Inside the baster was black mold. This didn't stop my mom from using it. But Robert stoutly refused to eat the turkey!

Robert got a good idea of the definition of cleaning at my parent's house after the phone rang on one occasion.

After a brief conversation, my mother hung up the phone. "Robert, help me pick up! Some friends just called and are coming over."

Robert looked bewildered. "How soon are they coming?" He was thinking they would need about a week.

"Oh, in just a few minutes."

Mom threw a few things behind the dresser and stuck a couple of Coke cans and an empty milk carton in a drawer. She threw something behind a door and shut the closet so her fifty wigs (all identical) would be out of sight.

"There. We're ready to go," she said with conviction. The company came and we left!

Amazingly enough, my mom ran a bed and breakfast out of her home. How she managed this or who stayed there still bewilders me. Robert was astonished when on one occasion she showed us the check a couple had given her. It had been cut out of a magazine and had VOID written on it. My mom accepted it.

During one afternoon visit, we walked into the kitchen and found Mom in a panic because she couldn't find a check she had been given.

"Your grandmother sent me a check for $5,000 and now I can't find it!"

She ignored us and continued to look for the money. Suddenly she yelled, "I found it!" Robert looked up to see her take it out of the refrigerator. It had been between the ketchup and the pickles.

"At least you know it won't be a hot check," Robert quipped.

Every time we left, Robert swore he would never go back. I knew it was just a matter of time before he would "gut it up" and go again. I could see that my parents were different but I was such a part of their warped thinking by now that I didn't recognize how bizarre their lives were.

My sister, Patty, and I developed our own way of dealing with the absurdities and thought we were handling everything well. Our humor kept us sane.

During one trip home, Patty and I both looked in the freezer for something to eat.

Patty picked up a package of meat and said, "I wonder how long this has been in here? Let's date it and check it next time we come."

We took a Marks-A-Lot out of the drawer and wrote 1/10/78 on it. We forgot about checking it until nine years later. The meat was still there!

7

PROVING MYSELF

As I got older, I desperately tried to get my parents approval, but because of their past pain and fears, they were not able to give out unconditional love. A person can't give out what they don't have. I applied this truth to myself also. I didn't have a lot to give out. I was empty. Control by intimidation or manipulation, whether it was verbal or physical abuse was all I knew. When conditions are put on love, the only way to receive it is by performing. I felt like I had to constantly be doing something important or I was not valuable.

Because the greatest value in my family was making money, I naturally set out to do the best I could in this area once Robert and I were married.

At the age of twenty-three, I bought a balloon wholesale/retail franchise which I ran for five years. It was a complete success in every way. I joined the Chamber of Commerce so that I could rub elbows with all the right people. My bank featured me on the front cover of their newsletter. Most of all I received validation from my family.

My grandmother sent me thousands of dollars to help me get started. Her pride was evident as she told everyone that I followed in her footsteps. Her "golden child" proved to be what she always wanted and hoped. Even my parents bragged about me to everyone. By all appearances, I was a bright and shining star. All, except, in the eyes of my husband.

"Penny, you are so wrapped up in this business. Is it really what you want to do or do you feel like you have to do it?"

"Of course it's what I want to do, Robert. I'd be bored to death just sitting around doing nothing. In my family, being ordinary is not allowed."

His voice lowered until I had to strain to hear his answer. "Ordinary is not so bad, Penny."

In spite of my protests to Robert, the truth of his words nagged away inside of me. Phrases my grandfather had said came back to me in my quiet moments.

"You shouldn't be named Penny. You're worth a million dollars."

"A person who is really successful doesn't do it for the money. Once you have enough to pay for the house and give yourself some security, you don't work for money anymore. Material possessions don't mean a thing to me."

Even though he said these things, he spent his whole life expending himself for money. Did I want to be like that? Did I want to be defined by how many dollars I could collect? I always needed more to prove myself. I began to see that something was not right in my perspective.

I also began to recognize that the friendships I made were very short-lived. I learned to reject others before they could reject me. I didn't like myself, so why would anyone else like me?

I found myself writing in my journal:

"I have made choices from examples modeled to me for years that have put me in bondage. Bondage is something a person finds himself in as a result of bad choices. The opposite of bondage is freedom and peace. The truth about who and what I have become is very disturbing. I don't feel free. I'm scared of what people think of me and I never feel like I fit in. I feel like there is this secret rulebook out there and nobody lets me read it. Everything I do seems to be wrong. I want to make excuses for myself but nothing I'd done so far has worked. I keep telling myself I am a good person. Why don't I feel good about myself then? Do I stay in denial? I am sick of having no true friends. I heard someone say recently that hurting people hurt people. I can't get this out of my mind. Why does this bother me so much? I can name a lot of hateful people who have hurt me. It's their fault and I didn't deserve to be treated badly. I want to blame them for my hurt!"

All my relationships ran about like this:

1. Meet someone who is an overall, nice person.
2. Find something in common with her.

3. Begin to get together on a regular basis.
4. Discover she sees something of value in my personality.
5. Recognize my faults but realize if she sticks around long enough, she will recognize them too.
6. Find it's too hard being honest so I break out the arsenal.
7. Overwhelm my newfound friend by making her the center of my hurt so she quits calling.
8. Excuse my behavior: "She's just jealous of me!"
9. Console myself: "I didn't like her anyway."

Recognizing these things about myself, I was beginning to long for a change in my life. Little did I know what was about to happen.

RULES

A principle of conduct observed by the members of
a group. A code of principles for the conduct
of religious services or activities.
—WEBSTERS DICTIONARY

8

THE PAIN GETS TOO GREAT

My daughter, Ashley, was three months old, my son a little over a year and I couldn't get my energy back. One night getting up with Ashley for her midnight feeding, I nearly passed out. Since my temperature was quite high, Robert insisted I see a doctor.

We sat in the lobby of the doctor's office with our two babies until they called me back to the lab to take a blood sample.

As soon as the physician walked into the room I asked, "Am I pregnant? I just know I'm pregnant!"

He looked at me stonily, impatience oozing out of every pore of his body. "I've been sitting in here with you for approximately three minutes, Ma'am. How in the world am I supposed to know the answer to that question?" His eyes squinted as he stared at me a moment longer. "I'll be right back."

Oh well, it's probably the flu. A few minutes went by when Dr. Personality walked back in.

"Ma'am, does cancer run in your family?"

What a question to ask! "I might have a dead aunt somewhere who had it."

Now I'm sure he was really impressed with me. He left the room again for about fifteen minutes. A small time under normal circumstances, but in light of his question, it seemed like an eternity, especially as I heard my daughter screaming in the lobby. I decided to go out and help my husband since I knew how exhausting it was to deal with her colic.

A nurse spotted me. "Don't leave that room!" Between Dr. Personality and the Wicked Witch of the West, I felt trapped.

The doctor finally returned. "There must be a glitch in the blood work machine."

"What's a glitch?"

"Well, your white blood cell count is very low, plus other counts are really off."

"What does that mean?"

"You're showing signs of leukemia."

The song, *Love Story*, began racing through my mind.

"You'll need to come back first thing in the morning so we can take some more blood."

I was numb. I don't remember the car ride home or walking though our front door. All I know is I immediately picked up the phone to call my mother.

"Mom, it's Penny. The doctors think they know what's wrong with me. It could be leukemia. I'm really sick."

I wasn't even surprised by her response. "We don't get sick."

"Well, I'm sick."

Dad got on the phone. "Hey, Penny, I have a friend who invented a cancer-detecting machine he's trying to patent. I've heavily invested in this (everything was always about making a dollar). He's an elder from church. We'll go tomorrow for a blood test with him. Once he puts you on this machine, we'll know whether it's cancer."

Hanging up the phone, I relayed all this to Robert.

Robert looked at me in exasperation. "This is bad news, Penny. Don't go to that crack-pot doctor."

I wasn't capable of listening to Robert so I went ahead. A few days later, this man called to say that his machine did indeed indicate that I had cancer.

I picked up the phone and called the first person that came to my mind, my preacher. I only knew God vicariously through other people. My preacher held the highest position of value, so somehow, he was my access to God. He came right over. I was an emotional wreck. I kept asking,

"Does God want me dead?"

Nothing I said was logical. Finally some words of wisdom came through to me. "If God wanted you dead, you would be dead! You have fallen into self-pity."

This man's words might have been harsh at the time but it is exactly what I need to hear.

Dad took me to my original doctor with the test results he had. This was his golden opportunity to sell this machine to the medical world. The doctor was actually pretty patient about the whole thing.

Six weeks later, I was referred to an oncologist/hematologist. "Please finalize what's wrong with me," I pleaded.

Checking into the hospital, I had a bone marrow test to see if I had leukemia. The test came back negative so I felt relief for a few days.

This whole experience did one wonderful thing for me. I was driven to the Bible for the first time in my life to find out what I believed or if I believed. The only time I saw the Bible being used was to prove someone wrong or to try to convert a person. For the first time in my life, I asked myself, *What's in the Bible that can change my life? How does this book apply to me?*

My husband went back to work and my kids went down for a nap. Life was back to normal, but I had a big job ahead of me. Looking beneath all the catalogues on our shelf, I found my Bible. I'd never opened a Bible to seek personal help until now. I introduced myself.

"My name is Penny and I have just had the hell scared out of me. I don't have a clue where to start and I have a lot of questions."

I just know I heard a voice. "My name is God and I have the answers."

My journals started to reflect a change in my attitude:

"For the first time in my life, I am asking myself what is in the Bible that can change my life? How does this book apply to me? I feel like I have been given a second chance at life, and this time, I'm not about to waste it." I wrote about a life changing experience in my journal a few weeks later:

"I sat down today and asked God to speak to me in a way I could hear Him and understand Him. I started my study in Matthew. I'm not quite sure how this is done but I'm willing to learn. The scripture in Deuteronomy 4:29 came to my mind. 'But from there you will seek the Lord your God, and you will find him, if you search after him with all your heart and with all your soul.' Well God, I'm seeking you with all I know to do. Do you really know

me? Do you know me as an individual? Do you even know my name or am I just another number to you? Please God, Show me you care! I opened up my Bible to where I had left off the day before and began to read in Matthew 10:29–31: 'Are not two sparrows sold for a penny? And not one of them will fall to the ground without your Father's will. But even the hairs of your head are all numbered. Fear not, therefore; you are of more value than many sparrows.'"

I could not believe it. My name, Penny, was right there. The name I had always been made fun of was not a joke to God. Then he went on to say, "fear not!" He has blessed me so much.

I cried and knew this friend I had met through the scriptures was bigger and more real than any earthly treasure I could obtain.

9

TURNING POINT

During all of the chaos going on in my life, I faithfully continued to attend church to make myself feel like I was doing something constructive to cover my pain. My thoughts churned as I wrote in my journal:

"How can I fix the mess I'm in? I have so many problems with my parents. I feel like people run the other way when they see me. If anyone calls or comes over, it's only because they want something from me."

I became desperate for change and would do anything to get the rules at this point in time. I went to my friend Sue Parr for help. She seemed to have order in her life and she was always kind to me. I knocked on her door.

"Hey Penny, come on in. I have coffee on."

"I don't want coffee, Sue."

When I turned down her offer for coffee she said, "Are you alright, Penny?"

"No, I'm not. I need you to tell me about this Bible study you're in."

"Sure, Penny. Sit down."

We spent the morning talking. She told me about an in-depth Bible study that I could attend with her. "It offers a way to not only understand the Bible but apply it to everyday situations."

I attended the study that week but there was a problem I had to work through once I started going. This study was extremely structured and because of my long association with rules at church, I had no trouble fitting in to this system. I, perhaps, fit into it too well.

I figured out early that in order to get into a leadership role, a person had to follow the rules strictly. I made sure that I never came to class without doing my lesson and never missed a class or came in late since that was considered less spiritual. If you didn't do your lesson, you weren't allowed to talk. Furthermore, you could only share what you had written down. I noticed women who were so fearful of disobeying the rules that they would write something down quickly, then raise their hand to speak. I wanted to fit in and win everyone's approval so I began to volunteer for everything. I stuck by the rules and didn't question a thing.

I can see now that I had been so conditioned by my dad to agree with his rules that I didn't know I had the freedom to make choices. I thought since an authority figure said it was a certain way, then it must be right. Since I was not allowed to question the rules as a child, my ability to become an individual had been squelched to the point of conforming. The problem is that rules become what people measure their self worth by. A person begins to judge himself and others according to how close they keep the rules and not according to how much they need grace.

This thought reflected my thoughts as I wrote in my journal:

"I didn't sleep well last night. Too much to process. I want to give this Bible study up. I'm doing everything I can to be accepted. I keep reading about peace in the Bible. There have been a lot of deep-rooted patterns ingrained in me since I was a child. This process of changing my ways is not going to be easy but I feel like I have taken the most important step of all, acknowledging to myself that I have some big problems. Denial is a fun place to be in as there is no responsibility. It's easy living and doesn't take work. The problem is, the consequences for my actions are constantly a barrier."

In spite of it all, this Bible study was a good thing for me. I had been searching for truth and was being stretched beyond my wildest dreams. I began to ask myself questions I never thought I was allowed to ask. I learned to make individual choices on what I viewed as valid and not what a certain group or person saw as valid.

This was reflected in my everyday life in many ways. At the video store one day, I ran into a person who had an important position in my church.

"Penny, have you seen this movie?"

"Yes, I have."

"I thought it was a great movie. Good acting, great plot. I liked everything about it. Did you like it?"

"Actually, no, I didn't."

This may not seem like a big deal, but for me this was huge. To disagree with someone who had a position that I deemed as important, without feeling the need to give an excuse was a big step for me.

After four years of hard work in this Bible study, I was asked into a leadership position.

"Penny, we think you would make a great group leader."

"Well actually, I've been praying about it and am certain that it would not be good for me."

"How can you possibly get an answer from God when you hadn't even been asked yet? We've been praying, too, and feel you would be a good leader."

"God speaks to me about my life before he speaks to anyone else about it. Actually, I have been working hard in order to be asked into leadership. This is exactly what I wanted but I wanted it because I need people's approval, not because I love to serve."

It was hard to make my honest confession but it was freeing too. I was beginning to realize that there was no group of perfect people and I didn't have to fit into some group to be secure in myself.

10

JOAN

The time change is always an adjustment for my family. We definitely like the "fall back" better than the "spring forward." I guess it wouldn't be so bad if it was Friday night instead of Saturday night. Getting to church on time is hard enough without the hour being messed up.

One particular daylight savings time literally changed my life forever. We had an extra hour so it was the perfect opportunity to turn over a new leaf. We were going to get to church early so we could sit downstairs, up front. No more balcony for us!

The whole family was in the car, ready to go and it was only 7:30 A.M. We got to church ten minutes early! I saw an empty pew close to the front where a man sat with his family.

Sitting down, I gave this man my biggest smile. "Hi! Boy, we're on the ball. Looks like you guys are too."

He smiled in return but didn't say much. When the service started, I continued to try to engage him in conversation.

"The songs are great this morning, aren't they?"

He smiled once more.

During the sermon I whispered, "Isn't he the best preacher?"

"Pretty good."

I was glad to get a response. After the service, I introduced myself. "I'm Penny Arnold and this is my husband, Robert."

"I'm Jess Arnold; nice to meet you."

"Wow, we have the same last name." I peeked over his shoulder. "Where did your family run off to?"

"Oh, that's not my family. I'm just visiting today. My wife and son are still in Florida, but I'm here with a new job. My motel is across the street so I thought I'd visit."

"Well, come home with us for dinner. It may be leftovers but at least you'll have company."

"I'd like that."

So Jess spent the day with us. A few weeks later, I met his wife, Joan.

I'm totally convinced that God put Joan in my path to show me what true friendship is all about. We hit it off right away because she laughed at my jokes. Going through a hard time herself, she needed my sense of humor. I knew when we met that she cared about me as a person. But what drew me to her most was her honesty. I needed someone who would tell me the truth because I was desperate to change my ways.

The wonderful thing about Joan was that she didn't judge me for all the inappropriate things I had done in the past. I had a fresh start with her. As I trusted Joan, she gave me a vision for what my life not only could but also would be.

I had only known Joan a couple of months when our friendship was put to the test.

"Joan, I bought tickets for a 'Tour of Homes' in Fort Worth to see the beautiful mansions decorated for Christmas. Come with me; you'll love it."

Joan gave me her *I'm trying to be patient* look. "Penny, I grew up in the Bronx with ten siblings. My dad died when I was three so my mom raised us all in a three-bedroom house. Practicality is my middle name and I'm not interested in looking at mansions."

"Oh, come on Joan. See how the other half lives. You don't have to move into one of these mansions, just see them."

She noticed the eager look in my eyes. "I guess we can go, but what's the point?"

"Well, for one we can get some great decorating ideas for Christmas."

"I'm living in a motel room, Penny. I don't think I'm going to be doing much decorating. But I'm also desperate to get out, so I'll go."

The day came and I cheerfully introduced her to my many "friends" who were working the tour. Halfway through when we hopped in the car Joan looked at me, annoyance on her face.

"Penny, these people are not your friends. I've been watching the way they treat you now for two months and that's not friendship! They use you for their purposes but they don't care about you."

I knew she was right. We didn't finish the tour but I began to ask myself what kind of person I wanted as a friend. Believe it or not, I'd never considered what was best for me before. I only took into consideration what position or group a person was in and let my surroundings and "skewed" views choose me. I didn't know how to choose a friend any other way.

I have since asked myself what is best for me? What do I want? A freedom I never experienced before has been the result. I have learned to say "no" to people based on an opinion I have, not an opinion I was told I should have.

True friends stick with you. Liz Bonham is one of those people. I met Liz when our children were two years old. I found out she liked to draw and I would go over to her house and see all her paintings. She was so gifted and told me never to give up on my dreams. Her dream was to display her art in different galleries. At the time it was only a dream but I have had the honor to walk with her in living it out. She has illustrated several books, including *The Crippled Lamb* by Max Lucado. She is constantly finding ways to give out to other people, including me. She was one of the few people who chose to be my friend and teacher rather than my judge. We have come a long way over the years and continue to enjoy our time together.

I found out early that Joan was not going to bail out on me either when I received an early morning phone call from her.

"Good morning, Penny. We're going to take a road trip."

"Oh really. Where?"

"Your parent's house."

Panic flooded through me. If she met my parents, I was in big trouble. "Why would you want to go there?" I asked lightly, hoping she'd change her mind.

"Because I have to find out if they are as bad as you say they are."

"I'll be there to pick you up in an hour. Okay, Penny?"

"Okay," I said warning her with a lilt in my voice.

I hung up the phone and two conflicting thoughts raced through my head. *What if my parents aren't as bad as I've made them out to be and Joan doesn't think it's that big of a deal? She'll think I'm a liar! On the other* hand, what if it's so bad she decides she doesn't want to hang around me anymore? For the first time, my parent's craziness worked in my favor.

She picked me up right on time.

I gave her instructions as soon as I got in the car. "We have to stop at the grocery store to pick up food for lunch before we go."

"Why? We'll be at your parent's house in a few minutes."

I began laughing uncontrollably so that I couldn't answer. She stopped to get gas but thought I was kidding about the grocery store so I had to insist again that we stop.

"Why are you laughing?"

I didn't know myself. Something about being around my parents sent me into gales of nervous laughter. Even the thought of it!

After arming ourselves with food, we walked up to the front door. Joan looked at the blue roach powder, shaking her head in wonder. I'll let her tell the story.

When we entered, both of Penny's parents were there, but neither one made eye contact with either of us. They did notice the grocery sack in my hand, however.

"What did you bring?" Her mom quickly took the sack from me, taking the food in the kitchen. Still with no introduction or interest in me, her dad began to complain.

"Why did you bring food? I made lunch!"

His first words were angry but then he began to withdraw, ignoring us totally. All the children were with us, but they never said a word to them.

I noticed that the more inappropriately her parents acted, the more Penny nervously laughed.

"Oh, roast beef!" Her mother happily unloaded the groceries. "I'd like a sandwich." She handed me a knife and let me get to work serving her first. I began to feed everyone. After eating, Penny announced that she and her mom were going shopping.

"You're going shopping now?"

"Yes. We'll be back in a little while. Here, I'll set up a video for you with the kids."

Clearing off the clutter, I sat down with the children. Even though I'd been raised in a family with ten children, I'd never seen so much dirt and mess. Just as we began to watch TV, her mom came back in.

"I had my money right where you are sitting. What did you do with it?" This was the first time she looked at me.

"*I have no idea what you're talking about,*" *I said shrugging my shoulders.*

She gave me one more suspicious look, then found it under the couch in a baggy.

After they left, I sat there with the kids wondering what I had gotten myself into. When they finally returned, I was very anxious to go. We gathered the children and packed up our things. Just as we reached the car, Penny's dad came out yelling.

"*You can't go yet! I need some duct tape.*" *He held up an empty tape roll.*

"*O.K., Dad. We'll get it.*"

Now I was really annoyed. "*Why did you tell him that? We've got to get back home.*"

"*It's no big deal, Joan. I know just what he wants. It will make him happy.*"

I agreed with a sigh but soon was exasperated as we went from one store to the other because we couldn't find the right kind of duct tape. I finally said, "*That's it, Penny. We are getting this one.*"

"*Okay, but I know it's not what he wants.*"

She was right. When she gave him the tape, he began waving his arms in the air, yelling, "*That's not what I wanted. What's wrong with you?*" *He then jumped into his Cadillac and squealed out of the driveway.*

All I could say on the way home was, "*You were not exaggerating, Penny. I've never seen anything like that.*"

Joan was convinced and our friendship survived.

11

HELP!

When I was eight months pregnant with my daughter, my grandmother had a stroke. It became evident that she would not recover. I flew to Arkansas to see her. Sitting next to her bed in the hospital room my mind began to go back in time. My mom walked in and the explosion began.

"Where's your checkbook, Mom. I've got to have it."

My grandmother looked at my mother with loathing in her eyes. "I hate you," she said.

"I need your checkbook and all your statements," Mom repeated.

My mom knew she wasn't the trustee of grandmother's estate and was well aware that she wasn't going to receive what she considered to be her fair share of the money. Mom had come into town a few days before I got there and while my grandmother was in the hospital dying, she went through her house looking for a copy of the will. When she found the will, it made her furious. She wasn't going to inherit all the money. My mom had only measured how much someone loved her by the price tag of the gift or the amount of money she was given.

As I continued to listen to their horrible banter, I thought, *my grandmother didn't like her mom, my mom doesn't like her mom, I don't like my mom and I'm carrying a daughter in my womb right now. What makes me think it's going to be any different for my daughter and me if something isn't done about this awful pattern that has been passed down for four generations?* My relationship with my parents had gotten out of control and I knew it, but I had no idea how to stop the madness.

The madness got worse over the next few years as I found myself journaling these thoughts:

"It is Thanksgiving and holidays around here have gotten to where I hate them! Robert and I got in another horrendous argument last night because I was telling him he needed to come with me to my parent's house today. He said, "No way, I'm not coming and that's the end of this discussion!"

Last Thanksgiving we separated, Robert going to his house and the kids and I going on to Dallas. Then Christmas, I came in with the kids to my parent's house and Robert came with me but in a separate car. He stayed for two hours at the most and then left to go to his parent's house, which is three hours away. I stayed at my parent's until late in the night and opened up gifts with the kids. Then I made the long drive to his parent's house. I found myself screaming, "Oh what fun it is to ride in a car shuffling kids all day!"

I thought, perhaps, my problem was solved when my parents moved to California. Dealing with them once a year would be all right. The phone call I received jolted me back into reality.

Dad was in his manic state and very persistent about being with my family on Thanksgiving Day. Twenty-four hours before or after that date was not acceptable and he let me know it. Trying to negotiate my schedule around all our families, the solution to me was to celebrate on different days since I knew my parents would be in town for two weeks. My dad became furious on the phone, totally unwilling to reason with me. When he began screaming into the receiver, I hung up.

This behavior was completely consistent with everything else my dad did but suddenly I'd had enough.

Pain will eventually motivate a person to act. This phone call was the straw that broke my camel's back. I contacted a therapist named Martha who turned out to be lifesaver for me. All the way there I thought, "This therapist better get me out of this mess I'm in. I've used up all my options and she's my last resort. If she tells me anything about working this thing out with my family, I'll run as far as the east is from the west. I know I need out."

When I met Martha, I felt like I had gone back twenty years. I became a little girl in my mind trying to explain where I was coming from.

I must have beaten the world record in how many words a person can say in one hour. I talked continually and felt like I was in the third grade. What I wanted most was to get out of my family.

"I never want to see them again, Martha. They are driving me crazy. I'm so confused; I feel that there is a secret rulebook out there but no one will let me read it. All I want are the rules!"

"I can't give you the rules, Penny, but I can be your guide. If you had cancer in your body, you would have no problem going to the doctor. He would do everything possible to help you rid your body of cancer. Think of me as that doctor."

Martha told me I needed to come back in a week and she had some ideas for me. She also said she wanted me to bring in someone else to tell her about my family. She said she needed another perspective.

I came back in with Joan and let her talk this time. Joan and I used up the whole session so I came back the next week with Robert. Martha said she didn't need anymore perspectives after that. She began her therapy sessions with me at this point explaining,

"Penny, all people are in different stages in life. Here's a simple illustration I have put together in the form of a ladder. On the bottom rung, I have written 'Chaos', above that is 'Rules', next is 'Ambiguity' and at the top is 'Peace'. Where would you say you are on this ladder?"

I had no trouble answering. "CHAOS, I'M IN CHAOS!"

"We are going to keep working until we arrive at 'Peace,'" she reassured me.

I left her office filled with hope. I didn't have to stay in chaos; what a wonderful thought. But the next time I talked to Martha, her words terrified me.

"You must confront your parents in person, Penny. They need to know that you are in chaos and that you have allowed them to keep you there. They have a right to know what is going on in your life."

"No way! My dad will lose it! I'm not the one with the problems, they are, so why do I have to make the first move?"

"It's your decision, but I don't think I can do much for you unless you take this step to describe your chaos and determine the steps needed to move out of it. It is a decision to take control over your own life."

I left her office upset and defeated. How was I going to face my dad? I had never been honest with him about my feelings. Looking back now, I can see I had blown this whole thing way out of proportion.

I realized that I couldn't go on like this. To stay in denial and protect our fragile shell of normalcy was ridiculous. Perhaps the hardest thing to recognize was that in being honest with my parents, I would be forced to be honest with myself about all the chaos.

I wanted to be on a level path. A roller coaster can be fun but trying to live on one is hellish.

I wrote this entry in my journal that night:

"I know I have to be up front with my dad. Could it be clearer than this? I don't think so! I need to do this but I am scared. Martha keeps asking me what am I afraid of? I can't answer that question. I want to be free from this root of rejection that has been sown in my heart. The only way I can heal and be free from the bondage I'm in is if I completely get out and be honest with all of them. A large part of the bondage I have been in is directly related to my staying involved with my family. It is time I make some hard choices. I have to break completely."

Later on that week I wrote,

"I looked up two words in the dictionary:

Malice—The desire to harm others or see others suffer.

Sincerity—Implies freedom from hypocrisy. A synonym for sincerity is wholeheartedly suggesting a total commitment and unstinting devotion to a cause.

I am not wanting to harm anybody or see anyone suffer but I am needing to be honest and free myself from pretending everything is okay with my family situation. I can't go on like this any longer. The ability to stay in denial to protect my reality can go to extreme measures. Thinking my situation is normal is extreme. I am taking my blinders off. I have been left with no choice. Confronting my parents will in turn, force me to confront myself."

I confronted my parents in Martha's office. For the first time in my life, I was honest with them (and with myself). I told my sister to come, too. My brother had made it clear that he did not want any contact with our parents or Patty, so I did not feel it necessary or even reasonable to invite him.

Patty, however, needed to be there. I would be able to find out for sure where she stood in all this. I needed to draw a line in the sand so to speak and know for sure if she was part of the problem I was facing, part of the cancer.

The chairs were positioned strategically in a circle. Mom seated herself in the 10:00 position, Dad at 2:00. Patty sat between our parents, which made me realize that she always took a mediator role.

As we began discussing things, my mom couldn't complete a sentence. Several times in the middle of a conversation, Patty would talk for her, at one point even saying, "Mama can't talk right now. I'm her interpreter."

I tried to explain to my parents why I was seeing a therapist. "My tools are broken so Martha is going to help me get a new set."

My dad's attitude was cocky immediately. "I'm just fine. I don't need new tools."

To further explain my illustration, Martha said to my father, "You would make sure you had a gun, for example, if you were going on a bear hunt. You wouldn't bring a broken gun would you?"

"Who needs a gun?" Dad threw his arms in the air, clenching his hands into fists. "I'm gonna fight the bear bare-handed!" I understood later that thinking he is invincible is consistent with being bipolar. My father received this diagnosis earlier but refused to take any medication to treat it.

No one could convince my parents or sister that anything was wrong or dysfunctional. I of course, had always been the black sheep of the family so needless to say, I was the one who was perceived to have the problem. Ironically enough, I was the one with the problem up until now. Mom and Dad said that the problem was that I was bitter and envious of their money. In fact, most of the conversation revolved around money.

"You are just jealous because you have to work and we don't." My dad said this with all confidence.

Mom stated at one point, "I loved you so much, Penny. I would have cashed in on you years ago because you were so cute."

I stayed focused. "Dad when you called the other day, it upset me because it wasn't about seeing me and my family for Thanksgiving. It was about you being in control and looking good on the holiday to portray a certain image."

"That's right. There's nothing wrong with that. Any other day *is* unacceptable. What does it say about how much you care about us?"

The conversation continued in this vein. I knew at this point that I needed to end the session since I had no power or tools to challenge my dad on his playing field. Amazingly, I left this encounter feeling relieved because it became apparent to me that it was impossible to discuss things with my parents. Even though I tried, I had no voice with them. They would not listen. By taking myself out of my parent's approval, I became free to explore my thoughts for the first time and find out who I really was and what I really believed.

Martha clarified this for me. "Some people have cancer and others have multiple sclerosis. A person can live with MS although it is uncomfortable and difficult to cope with. Cancer, on the other hand, will kill you if it is not treated. You must decide what your family is to you, MS or cancer."

This session made it clear to me that I needed to remove myself from my parent's influence and get the help I needed.

Because of this, not blaming my parents for my problems has been a major hurdle to clear. I forgave them, but have not reconciled to them. I have also come to realize over time that my parents are mentally ill and staying in the chaos would have made it impossible for me to get well.

The next time I met with Martha, she had another visual illustration to show me. It was in the form of a pie divided into five pieces. One piece had "Hero" written on it, the next, "Scapegoat", then another, "Comic", next, "Peacemaker" and the last, "Lost child."

"Penny, I've been thinking about your situation. Every dysfunctional family has different players and these are the names for them. What role do you think you play in your family?

"The Comic. I'm the funny one."

"Hmm." That was all she said. I thought she meant I got it wrong so I changed my answer.

"Well, maybe it's the Peacemaker."

"You are *not* the Peacemaker!" She was emphatic about this.

I shrugged my shoulders, "I guess I'm the Scapegoat."

"Hmm."

At this point I was getting frustrated, so I took the illustration from her and studied it for a moment. "I know I'm not the Hero . . . Lost child?" I looked at her dubiously.

Suddenly the lights came on. I smiled broadly. "It really doesn't matter what the answer is, Martha, because I'm not in it any more!"

Martha smiled. As soon as the words were out of my mouth, I knew this was key to my situation.

12

THERAPY

Because my family had grown up with so many secrets, I went to the opposite extreme, telling everybody anything they wanted to know (actually way beyond what they wanted to know.) I thought I was breaking a pattern but all I was doing was creating a new unhealthy pattern. A friend once commented, "Penny, you say you don't trust people, so why do you tell everyone everything about yourself?"

Her question perplexed me. I asked Martha why she thought I did this. "It is common for those who have grown up with some kind of dysfunction to want to break the pattern by doing the exact opposite thing their parent did. The trouble is they may be doing something that is just as destructive because they simply trade one unhealthy pattern for another. For example, a person whose parents were very controlling may marry someone exactly the opposite in his determination never to be controlled again. However, he then becomes the controller, repeating the pattern."

With this awareness, I became more careful in whom I confided. I made sure that when I told someone something I had a purpose in mind and not just to unload on unsuspecting people I ran into.

Martha continued to challenge every area of my life. In one of our early sessions, she asked about my jewelry. "Do you always wear your jewelry?"

"Yes. Always."

"Think about that, Penny."

"What's there to think about?" I wondered.

Her question plagued me for a month. I started asking myself questions. *Why does it matter to me that I wear my jewelry? I've given away some very expensive jewelry to someone I truly loved. If I were being materialistic, I certainly wouldn't be giving my jewelry away.*

Satisfied with my line of reasoning, I presented it to Martha. She was not convinced.

"Are you willing to take a test for the next few months?"

"Sure, why not?"

"Take off your jewelry."

"That's no big deal. I'll do it."

Feeling vulnerable and worthless, it amazed me how uncomfortable I was without my jewelry. The next time I saw Martha, I protested.

"I don't see what I'm supposed to be learning from this."

"Could it be that you are wearing diamond studs as a crutch?"

I sat there in silence knowing that my jewelry gave me the false illusion that I'm better than other people and was a cover-up for my pain.

I sighed, pausing just a moment before answering.

"You're right."

Jewelry had become so much a part of who I was that it became normal to use it to intimidate people. I had to learn a whole new way of relating to others.

In elementary school, I broke my right wrist so I had to learn to eat with my left hand. Uncomfortable and frustrated, I would have to stop to rethink how to make the number 5 or the letter S. Every stroke of my pencil took concentration. It felt much the same now.

My children have been my best teachers. So many everyday experiences have become lessons in relearning how to live.

"Mom, I need some pantyhose." My seven-year-old son looked up at me with his big, brown eyes.

"Why in the world would you need a pair of pantyhose?" I had to admit his question bothered me quite a bit. No seven-year-old should need pantyhose!

"It's for the reindeer we're making at school. We shape wire into a what looks like his head and then stretch the pantyhose around it."

Okay, crisis over.

After wandering around the grocery store a while, I asked a young man stocking the shelves.

"Where are the hose?"

"Oh, aisle 7."

Easy enough, I thought. But in aisle 7 when I found the lawn and garden section, it dawned on me that he thought I meant a garden *hose*.

I finally found the right aisle and took the pantyhose to the checker.

"Ma'am, these are small. Are you sure that's the size you need?"

No, I wanted extra-large. It's good you don't work on tips, I thought, but I patiently replied.

"They're for my son."

Before I could explain, the man behind me said, "Don't tell Dad."

As I left I thought of all the different videos running in people's heads.

I asked Martha, "How do you get years of videos out of your mind?"

"You have to change the filter you view it through."

This may seem like a simple answer but it was just what I needed to hear. Until now I always thought the world was an extension of me. If I saw things a certain way, surely everyone else did too. I'd judge others by my own selfish motives, which caused me to view the world in fuzzy focus. I was sure everyone evaluated my worth by what car I drove, the house I lived in, or what I wore.

Only capable of looking at a situation according to my own damaged perception, I would judge a person with money, for example, as materialistic. If that person crossed my path, I'd become intimidated and they wouldn't know what hit them because I would use all my sick weapons, either bringing up something about my family money or drawing attention to my jewelry. I hadn't owned my sin of materialism; therefore, I wasn't capable of believing anyone else had either. When judgement gets in the way, I can no longer love.

How completely I was wrapped up in my own view of things was even reflected in the way I read the Bible. In Numbers 26:2 I read that God told Moses, "Take a census of all the congregation of the people of Israel, from twenty years old and upward, by their father's houses, all in Israel who are able to go forth in war."

I couldn't believe it. From the little knowledge I had been taught, there were at least three million people involved here. How in the world could Moses count that many people? I really began to get nervous for Moses.

God needs this information, I thought. *If you blow this one, Moses, God is going to have the wrong number!* I kept reading the passage over and over. Then it hit me. *God doesn't need this information. He already has it. God doesn't need your help with anything.* I was beginning to see how far my self-centered thinking went!

13

X-RAY VISION

In fifth grade, I subscribed to *Mad Magazine*. Somehow this seems an appropriate periodical for me to have received then. In the back were various advertisements directed toward the naïve , or should I say, vulnerable, customer. I fit into this category, getting hooked quickly on these ads. The one that got my attention and my money was a pair of x-ray glasses. My imagination soaring about seeing through doors and such, I parted with ten dollars, licked the stamp, sealed the envelope and mailed it off.

Everyday for what seemed a year, I would check the mail anxiously. It finally came! I opened my ten-dollar prize only to find a pair of plastic glasses with snaps on both sides of the rims. Included were twenty circular cardboard cutouts with pictures printed on them that I could snap onto the glasses. The instructions said to choose the picture that best fit the scene I was looking at. On the bottom of the instructions were the bold letters, NON-REFUNDABLE. I wonder why?

My perception of how things should be growing up was a lot like those glasses. I have so many memories that are good but I also have some it would be nice to snap a different cutout over.

I found out through counseling that my family was enmeshed, meaning no one had a separate identity; we were all one. The mystery behind my bizarre behavior was being exposed for the first time. I was repeating the only behavior modeled to me and because of the enmeshed situation I was in, I had taken on the characteristics of my parents as if I were them because there was no separating any of us.

My father's personality exhibited extreme highs and lows in his emotions. It caused me to be very insecure because I didn't know what he was going to do a lot of the time, especially in public. A book that was instrumental for me was *On the Edge of Darkness* by Katie Cronkrite.

My therapist suggested I read it to better understand the diagnosis of the manic-depressive disorder. This book helped me connect with the part of my father I never could seem to understand. It gave several stories of well-known people who either lived with someone or had this mental disorder. As I began to read what deep pain a person is in when they hit the extreme highs and lows, I began to understand the shame and embarrassment they have after different episodes occur due to their behavior. Without medication, the crazy incidents keep happening. A chemical imbalance does not go away on its own. Convincing the bipolar to get on and stay on medication can be very difficult. When people with this disorder reach an extreme high, they actually think they are indestructible and don't need any help. The lows they experience can make them suicidal. It can be a vicious cycle.

Since my parents have not been interested in admitting that they have a problem and need to seek help, it has become necessary for me to place limits on their need to control me for their own selfish motives. Because I had nothing to draw on from my past to reassure myself that my new way of doing things was not going to get me in bigger trouble, I looked at the people's lives I was looking to for guidance. I asked myself, *Is his life producing positive results? How is his life impacting others? Are other people growing because of his counsel?* If I could answer "yes" to these questions, I kept going forward with confident assurance that what I wanted was going to happen. I had to be certain that what I hoped for was waiting for me in the future even if I couldn't see the big picture at that point in time.

My old familiar ways were comfortable and even though they continued to put me right back where I started, the end result was predictable. This made me feel like I could at least control the results. My new ways of doing things felt uncomfortable, but I would tell myself that the old ways weren't bringing me peace as a result so how could it hurt to experiment with something different. I had nothing to loose. I was determined to find peace as I faced my jumbled past.

14

THE DOMINO EFFECT

For my own mental health and for the sake of my children I decided I would not budge on my decision to have no further contact with my parents or my sister. I was prepared to use physical distance for my protection.

If I knew there was something in my environment making me physically ill, I'd change my surroundings. My parents were making me mentally unhealthy so I had to separate myself from them in order to get well.

Within a month my parents sent gifts for my children, which was not consistent with their character. In fact, the previous Christmas, my daughter asked for an Easy Bake Oven. Mom told me to go ahead and purchase it and that she would reimburse me. I gave it to her from my mother but never received the money. This was typical.

The only thing that was consistent was that they were trying to use money to solve things. On the outside it seemed a nice and loving thing to do but it was clearly pure manipulation on their part. I opened the gifts and gave them to my children.

Enclosed in the package was a poster in bold letters; it stated *Love is Patient; Love is Kind*, etc. I thought to myself, *I love my husband and children enough to stay away from any poison that could hurt them. It is my responsibility to keep my family safe. Love does not mean that I roll over and allow my parents to walk all over me while I pretend things are peachy keen. Setting boundaries for myself is actually a very clear sign of love. I love myself enough to keep my power or in my case, get my power back. I admit that I have problems with my family and have begun to release myself from denial, which in turn gives me the power to make choices that are healthy. I take responsibility for my situation and am pro-active for the first time. I have been the one all along setting up the expectations in this relationship. How can my parents be healthy grandparents if they aren't healthy parents to me?* I was beginning to leave the chaos.

As I watched my children play with the toys, I grew angrier by the moment. My stomach actually hurt, so I packed up the toys and sent them back to my parents. I realize now that this was not what I should have done. By reacting to my parents hurt, I gave them the power. The only control I have over an unexpected circumstance is my response to it. The best response would have been to give the gifts away to someone who would appreciate them and leave my parents out all together.

A few months later I received an anonymous package with all my photos and my children's photos in it. Old letters I had sent to my aunt, mom and dad were also included. As I leafed through them, I noticed phrases from my dad such as, "how much I love my only two grandchildren" and that they were "the apple of my eye." My dad was not trying to reconcile. This was battle; I would win!

I continued to see my counselor and knew she was a very strong link in my setting and maintaining my boundaries. A support system at this point was a must and my desire to get healthy had to be extremely strong.

There were more attempts at breaking down my boundaries I had set up. I was not going to let their behavior change my course of action.

My aunt called and started in, "Penny, what kind of person calls themselves a Christian and then cuts off her mom and dad? What about your responsibility to them and to your sister?

"I'm sorry you don't understand, but I can't continue to be part of their dysfunction. I'm not capable of contacting anyone in my family right now."

"That sounds pretty selfish. Patty is very upset and not doing well at all because of this. You've hurt her."

This was the hardest, but I somehow got through the conversation and off the phone. When I shared this with Martha, she helped clear things up for me.

"So, your sister's happiness depends on *your* decisions and *your* actions? That's a pretty big responsibility to take on, Penny."

I also learned that guilt messages are really anger in disguise. Martha made me see at this point that no matter what I did was not good enough for my family. It is not about me. Healthy people do not force their opinions or beliefs on other people. They respect other people's boundaries and "no" is not a threatening word.

A little over a year passed before I heard from any member of my family. Patty called.

"Penny, don't you think we could get together and work this out?"

"I'd be glad to get together, Patty. But I'd like my therapist there. Also, it needs to be between you and me without Mom and Dad."

In a shocked tone of voice, she responded, "How could we not tell Mama and Daddy?" Needless to say, we didn't meet.

The next call was from my aunt, left on our answering machine. "Your dad is going in for triple bypass surgery, Penny. I thought you should know." She proceeded to give me all the details.

I chose not to see my dad, and it was not a difficult decision. Confident that I was not responsible for my dad, I did not need to do anything. That day I came to terms with the fact that we will probably never reconcile. A few days later I received another phone call letting me know the surgery went fine. My aunt added that some of this came on because of stress and that I should think about that. I refused to. I am not responsible for his stress.

All my life I had taken on other people's problems that weren't mine to begin with. Then I would feel like I needed to go around and try to explain myself. I would waste my time trying to fix their situations. People without boundaries feel the need to be understood and seek approval and affirmation from other people. I finally decided I didn't owe my aunt or any person on this earth an explanation. This wasn't my problem and I wasn't going to take it on! My aunt hung up mad. I kept my power.

15

EVERYTHING IS MADE NEW

I had to reevaluate almost every aspect of my life, finding out quickly that most things needed radical change. First was evaluating the people I spent time with because this impacted me the most.

As reflected in my journal at this time, I wrote:

"I have been accused of being a cut-off person in several areas of my life. It seems this new road I am going down requires me to think differently using new strategies in order to gain the freedom and peace I so long for. I'm not going to get these results by following the old familiar ways that once ruled me. By making different choices, I'm finding out that the end results are true joy and that is my reward."

I thought about where I wanted to be in the next five years. On a piece of paper I made two columns. One side, I titled *What this person has to offer me*, the other *What I have to offer this person*. Then I wrote down every person I could think of.

This was necessary because of my old pattern of choosing friends according to their position or influence in society. Having spent a lifetime going about it the wrong way, I wanted to do it right this time. The chart helped me understand who in my circle of acquaintances were true friends who would be honest with me and point me toward my need for peace. I also needed people who would believe in me rather than use me. On the other hand, I also needed to come clean with those people in my life that I used for my selfish purposes as well.

There is a story about a boy who played golf with his dad and always ended up with a terrible game since his dad would criticize and ride him the entire time on the golf course. When a friend of his father's invited him to play with him, this boy made a hole in one, and his overall score was lower than it had ever been.

"Why do you have such a bad game with your dad every time you play? You're great!"

The boy looked up at him. "When I'm with you, nothing is expected of me."

Another word for this story is grace. It frees us to be who we are rather than what others expect us to be. I desperately needed people in my life who would be gracious to me.

Along with my relationships, I was involved in a myriad of activities. To sort through all of these, I wrote down all the activities I was doing. I asked myself questions, which required honest answers. "Why was I involved with a particular activity or responsibility? It was critical that I be honest with myself because my whole life had been centered on getting somebody's approval. I learned early that the way to get approval was by pleasing people. Another harsh way to put it is, I had always "prostituted myself out" to other people. It didn't matter if the work was good and respectable. I'm still allowing myself to be used if I'm busy trying to get approval from people. My life continually turned into a *"Let's pretend I'm a good person"* game. Filling my days with anything that gave me a false sense of well being left me firmly planted in fantasy world.

When Robert and I went to Walt Disney World for our fifteenth wedding anniversary, a voice came over the speakers as we rode the monorail.

"Attention passengers. If you will look out the right side of your window, you will see the castle entrance to the Magic Kingdom. We actually have people who book their weddings in this magical spot to start their marriage underneath the beautiful, mystical castle."

Robert looked at me with a smirk. "Great, just what every healthy couple needs, a marriage starting off in fantasy land!"

I was ready for reality. As I wrote down my everyday activities, I was startled by what I found. Many of the things I was involved in, I'd started seven to ten years ago for all the wrong reasons. It was radical for me but I dropped out of most of these activities so that I could start with a fresh slate, making wise decisions that reflected what I was designed to do and not because someone else told me to do it. As I enter new responsibilities now, I constantly ask myself, *"Is this working?"* If not, I change what I'm doing. I was learning to be proactive when it came to governing my life instead of reacting to circumstances as they came along.

The dominoes just kept falling. At this time, my husband and I decided to leave the church we were raised in. This denomination was all we knew and a huge part of our lives. As adults, Robert and I had never stopped to ask ourselves why we were in this particular church but stayed only because it was familiar. In all the years I'd attended, I never felt free to ask questions about why and how we did things. In fact I was afraid to do so. Like so many other areas of my life, I did what I did because I'd been told to.

Robert and I were discovering grace, feeling a peace about who we were for the first time in our lives. We were discovering that God loves us not because of our character but because of His character. Leaving the only church and belief system I knew was my way of owning my faith. It gave me the strength and courage to break out of the box I felt locked up in all my life.

I was still dealing with hang-ups about money. I knew this was a pitfall but I kept falling into it over and over. If someone had something I perceived as better than mine, I felt threatened. The same was true of anyone who had better accomplishments or seemed to be well liked. I had no self-confidence so I felt the need to prove myself all the time. I could make myself believe that if I only had that new outfit, then I could impress others enough so they would like me. If they didn't like me, at least they would be jealous of me which gave me a false sense of power.

I tried hard once again to do something about my view of money. In an effort to break my materialistic outlook, I volunteered at a food pantry. After finishing there one day, I went straight to my appointment with Martha.

"Boy, am I glad I'm not like the people that come in there! It's awful."

Martha looked at me, pausing thoughtfully. I knew I'd said something that would spur her on to ask me questions!

"Penny, imagine that everyone is born on a huge stairway with three hundred steps. You may have been born on step number 235 and someone in that food pantry may have been born on step number 5. What do you think each person's responsibility is on the stairway?"

I stared blankly at her not seeing the point she was trying to make.

Patient as always, she began to explain, "Where we are on the stairs is not important, only that we are taking the next step up. That's all that's required."

We talked about this concept the rest of the session, light dawning as I began to understand.

Relationships, activities, money, and church all had to be reconsidered, but so did my physical well being. After having my two children, I put on so much weight that I was 210 lbs. Through some effort, I dropped to 165 lbs. but knew I was still quite a bit overweight. Through a program called "Weigh Down Workshop" by Gwen Shamblin, I learned to stop eating in order to get my emotional needs met. I lost thirty pounds and have kept it off ever since. There are still days I struggle with wanting to eat when I'm not hungry, but being aware of the problem is half the battle.

I love to work out, especially running with my friend. Over time, she developed a sore knee. In spite of wrapping it with a bandage, it wasn't getting any better.

"How long has it been since you bought new running shoes?"

"A long time. I've had these forever."

"That could be your problem. Try buying some new shoes to see if that helps your knee."

Sure enough, new shoes were all she needed. Her knee felt just fine after that.

I share this to illustrate how I "covered up," "fixed up," and even said I was on the "up and up," when what I was actually doing was continuing to "mess up" because the root of my problem had not been dealt with. This was the story of my life but everything was rapidly changing now.

AMBIGUITY

"Susceptible of multiple interpretation. Doubtful or uncertain, lacking clarity of meaning. The presence of two or more possible meanings."
—WEBSTERS DICTIONARY

16

COLOR MY WORLD GRAY

I always wanted Martha to give me the rules. Because my dad had controlled me, I looked to her to do the same. I thought that if someone who was healthier than my parents called the shots, I would be okay. When I married Robert, I looked to him to do that, which he tried to do. Now I was looking to Martha. Everything was so easy if I just knew what to do.

The only problem was that Martha stoutly refused to do this. "My job, Penny, is to pull from you what you believe you should do. E.E. Cummings said, 'He who asks a more beautiful question gets a more beautiful answer.' That's my role, to ask the questions."

"Well, I've been coming to you for three years now and you told me you would be my guide, but I just don't feel like I'm getting a map from you."

"Where will the map go?"

"I don't know."

"When you get it, the map will go further than I can take you."

This was hard because I had to decide what was right, rather than be told a pat answer. I began to make decisions tentatively, looking to Martha for praise to see if I made the right choice. She again refused to do this, leaving the decision entirely to my discretion. I now see that she was teaching me to be a grown-up. I had learned to realistically face the chaos that I was in and had ordered my life accordingly. Now I was being stretched in new ways. I found out that I couldn't live life by just following the rules I'd laid out for myself. There were all sorts of gray areas that required me to think about each case individually.

Martha illustrated the stage I was in by asking me questions from a story.

"Imagine a ghetto where kids are killing each other for their tennis shoes or hub caps. You have been asked to make sure that the killing stops immediately. How would you do that?"

I answered, "I would go in with Law to achieve Order."

"So, you would make clear rules that everyone had to follow?"

"Yes, I would take away any weapons they had to prevent their killing, and I would impose a curfew whereby no one could be out after dark when I couldn't see them."

Martha continued, "Six months pass with no killings and a little girl asks if she can go to say goodbye to her dying grandmother who lives too far away to get back before dark. Will you rigidly impose your rule or will you make an exception?"

"I will let her go".

"So what happens to the rule when everyone finds out you bent it for this one?"

"It's no longer black and White; we know there are some gray areas."

I could see through her illustration that I was entering that stage. Interestingly enough, it started with a small item like shoes.

I have always said that I hate shoes. Of course I wore shoes when I had to, such as at church or out to eat, but any other occasion, I went barefoot. My dear friend, Liz, eventually became curious about that.

"Why are you always barefoot, Penny?"

"Growing up in Colorado, I never wore shoes much so I developed thick calluses on my feet. Rocks, snow, whatever, didn't bother me. I just don't need shoes."

The fact was that I always owned only two pairs of shoes: a white pair of tennis shoes and a pair of simple brown flats. These would be replaced only when they were falling apart.

On a shopping trip with my son to purchase new shoes for him, I noticed a pair of women's clogs. I kept walking by them telling myself that they were very interesting. Then I'd think to myself, *Oh well, I don't like shoes.* While my son spent thirty minutes trying to decide which shoes to pick, I spent the entire time telling myself why I didn't like those clogs. I finally realized how ridiculous this was and took the plunge in purchasing them.

A few weeks later, I found a pair of blue suede sandals I liked. Again, the argument began with myself, but it only took ten minutes to decide this time. Finally, I got to the point where I could buy a pair of shoes without thinking twice about it. I kept asking myself why I had to make such a big deal out of such a simple thing. People *like* shoes, people *buy* shoes, people even *wear* shoes! After a few days it hit me like a ton of bricks what this was all about.

The memories came trickling back about how my mother would always buy me the same "black softies" year after year. Since I couldn't pick out what I wanted, I decided that I didn't like shoes at all. As I got older, I never questioned why I developed this belief. It took me all these years to break through that pattern to discover why I behaved as I did.

There were other things that happened to me as a child that have stayed with me as an adult.

I wanted some gum from the store. My mom said "no" but that didn't stop me from saying "yes." I stole a piece of gum, stuck the wrapper in my pocket and popped the gum in my mouth. When we got in the car, the flavor I chose must have given me away.

"What's that smell?" my sister asked.

My brother took one look at me. "Penny has gum, Mom!"

My mother immediately turned around to look at me in the back seat. "No wonder you didn't fight with your sister for the front seat. Where did you get that gum?"

I swallowed the evidence. "I don't have anything in my mouth."

She leaned over the seat, taking the corner of the gum wrapper out of my pocket. "What's this then?"

I began to wail, "It's Mike's fault! If he hadn't told on me nobody would have known."

My logic was that if I didn't get caught, it wasn't wrong. My mom made me go back into the store to tell the store manager what I'd done. He said he wouldn't take me to jail this time, but next time he would, so I'd better not do it again. It made a deep impression.

I was working through other gray areas, which became apparent when I felt I could wear my diamond necklace because I liked it and not because it proved something to others. Martha noticed me wearing it one day, but said nothing. She left the room for a few minutes and when she returned, I had tucked the necklace under my shirt. She didn't mention it until much later, but it showed me the shaky steps I was taking. I was able to break the rules, but not very confidently.

I began to question the rules when it came to parenting my children as well. I laid enormous expectations on them and took a lot of pride in their accomplishments. My son won numerous awards for academics, which filled me with pride. I often heard, "So you are Josh's mom. You must be so proud!" I was, which I let Josh know in no uncertain terms. The night of the Awards Ceremony, I thought joyfully of attending so that everyone could see how bright my son was. However, I found out that he in no way wanted to attend because he did not want the awards to define him. I gave up my dreams of adulation in his accomplishments for his sake, so we skipped the Awards Ceremony and went out to eat instead. This was about him, not about me. I could see I was making progress as I chose to value my son over the awards.

My human nature still compels me to do what is right because I don't want to pay the consequences; however, my thinking today has changed to some degree. I was designed to find peace and one way this is achieved is by choosing good over evil.

When I was in elementary school, my science teacher took us all out on the playground. He was trying to illustrate to us the laws of nature and gravity. We were asked one at a time to stand behind this white line and in front of us was a heavy ball hanging from a rope.

"Step up and pull the ball right up to your nose without touching it to your face and then let go of the ball."

The teacher continued, "Now, do not move from the position you are in because you are not allowed to dodge the ball."

One by one we all participated in this experiment and every one of us dodged the ball.

The teacher was trying to get us to see that gravitational pull will not allow the ball to come back any farther than it was originally let go to begin with.

This story applies to me today. Everything has equal force. The bigger my mess up, the bigger consequence I will have to face!

A person will pay a bigger price for murder than the person who gossips; however, there are a couple of things these people have in common. Both are robbed of their peace and both need grace just the same."

17

TRIANGLES

Being in the color gray caused me to ask questions. A lot of them! Being in this stage also required me to come up with answers and apply them to tough situations I was now facing. There were old problems that now required new solutions.

I never learned healthy ways to deal with my pain and so I allowed my feelings of being rejected to manifest into anger which began to take over my life. Anger is easier to deal with than pain because it gives one a false sense of power. Anger is one of three things: Hurt, frustration or fear. I now ask myself when I become angry, "Which emotion am I trying to deal with here?" I can take control at this point and reason with myself. When I give in to anger, I become illogical because I haven't figured out why I'm angry.

However, it is important not to side step the anger stage of grief. If anger is not dealt with properly then the anger will never go away. Anger does not know time so if a person doesn't face what's been done to hurt them, then the anger will never go away. It becomes old anger.

Getting the right perspective to the problem will help in getting a hands-on solution. I have found that most of the time, going directly to the source of a gripe I have is the best way to confront my own emotions.

I had a long, ongoing dispute with a person and the problem wasn't going away on its own. I had always told a mutual friend of ours about the problems in this relationship but my gossiping was starting to bug me. When things didn't seem to be changing I told Martha about the problem.

"I have asked Sarah to get out of the middle of this on-going problem. She continually gets involved anyway. How can I get her out of the middle?"

"Penny, how can she get out of the middle when you are the one constantly putting her there?"

I didn't have the tools to be honest with this third party. It was now my responsibility to face this problem head on.

When the opportune time came I talked with the person I had a problem with. I was up-front with her and told her my destructive patterns were only causing more conflict.

The relationship didn't change but something much more important did. I no longer involved other people in a conflict that wasn't theirs to begin with.

Being honest gave me a sense of self-respect and power over owning my feelings. I was showing myself that I had integrity as well. I didn't need to hide behind my friend, and I was no longer hurting this third person when she received second-hand information.

Truth about who we are and what we have become is critical in order to grow up in maturity.

18

SEEING THROUGH DIFFERENT EYES

As a friend of mine looked through my photo album, I caught myself trying to explain one of those Kodak moments of my daughter blowing out the candles on her birthday cake. In the snapshot, she looked happy and excited. We were both all smiles.

Seeing the picture, my friend commented, "What a fun day."

"Oh, that's just the snapshot. You should see the video!"

The video told the true story. Ashley wanted the knife we were using to cut the cake. Since I wouldn't let her have it, she pitched a fit. Nothing would make her happy except that knife. Finally, we let her have a dull, plastic knife so she could cut a small piece of cake. We captured her smiling and happy for a few brief moments in the photograph.

So it is with the way we judge each other. We get a small glimpse of a person's actions, what he said or how he reacted to a situation. This causes us to draw a whole lot of conclusions that we decide are fact. We even say things like, "I've got him pegged," never realizing that we don't know the whole story.

A perfect example of this was a recent incident as I looked around for a familiar face in the auditorium I was in one night. I spotted my best friend's husband, Jess Arnold. When I sat down, he explained that Joan was dropping off their son at his class and I told him Robert would join me shortly.

We fell silent as the speaker began. "I'd like you all to stand and meet those around you. Introduce yourselves and make everyone feel welcome."

Jess and I stood up as a couple we had never met greeted us.

"Hi, we're Kathy and Joe Smith."

"I'm Penny Arnold."

"I'm Jess Arnold; nice to meet you."

I immediately felt the need to explain. "We're not married."

Jess gave me a look like, *Penny, don't try to explain.*

Another couple met us. "Hi, we're the Moores."

"Hi, I'm Penny Arnold."

"Jess Arnold. Pleased to meet you."

I told these people that we had the same last name but we weren't married. I could see Jess out of the corner of his eye pleading, *Blow it off, Penny.* So when a third couple introduced myself, I let it go with no explanations.

The service started and three minutes later Robert sat down next to me, put his arm around me and whispered in my ear. I could imagine the couple behind us thinking we were a very liberal couple! They thought they had all the facts.

My son and I were enjoying a pleasant moment together drinking a Coke when his voiced piped up, "Look, Mommy, a telescope!"

He had one eye closed as he peered through his straw, focusing on the image he could see through the narrow passageway. He gleefully told me everything he could see through this small hole.

When he put the straw down, I asked him what he now saw. Of course there were many things he missed before.

We make assumptions and judgements by what we see through our narrow straw. We're not capable of seeing the big picture.

All this time, I continued to see my therapist. I felt sad for her when her husband died unexpectedly. I wanted to honor her with my time and appreciation by attending the funeral because of all she had done for me. When I arrived, I was in complete shock. Never in the entire time I had been seeing her did she drop a name about her circle of friends. When I pulled up to the grave site, I was given a program listing the people who would be speaking that day which included James Dobson,

Chuck Swindoll, Barbara Johnson, and Ann Graham Lotz. A letter from Pat Robertson was read and Max Lucado gave the closing prayer. These men and women held back tears as they described Martha's husband and his walk with the Lord.

Just a few years before my grandfather died. There were a lot of "important" people at his funeral, too. I have a letter from President Reagan that was read at the funeral. Many business tycoons were there and almost everyone spoke about how much money he had. I heard numerous stories about how my grandfather "wheeled and dealed" in his prime and how clever he was when it came to making a dollar.

I thought of the thousands of people that got involved with my grandfather's business. Stories came back to me that spoke of people that were used or hurt along the way because of the power behind this man's money. He influenced people all over the country but the person I feel the most pain for is my mother. His influence on her, in turn, affected her children.

I couldn't help but notice the juxtaposition between these two men's funerals. The similarities between the two looked the same on the outside, but one man chose God and the other, the world. It compelled me to ask myself who is more important to me; God or men. I realized that how I answered that question would not only affect me, but all the people I share my life with. As I've moved from hard and fast rules to meeting others with grace, I find I have the "peace that passes all understanding."

PEACE

The absence of war or other hostilities. Freedom from
quarrels and disagreements; harmonious relations.
"They made peace with each other." Inner contentment,
calm, serenity; peace of mind.
—WEBSTERS DICTIONARY

19

IS YOUR POWER ON?

An essential quality for freedom and peace is the willingness to admit when you're wrong and a commitment to change no matter what.

Peace is when I give up my self-made agendas. I can no longer figure it out, control it, fix it, justify my ways, talk about it or worry about it. Peace is going forward—believing everything has a purpose when logic says it makes no sense.

My journals began to reflect the feeling of peace as I wrote:

"I was at my friend's house last night, which is about three miles away from mine. As I got something out of my purse, I came across our garage door opener, accidentally hitting the control button. For an instant I thought my garage door was going to go up. I quickly realized that it only works when I'm within a certain range of the door. How true of my personal walk. I have the control switch in my hand. I have the power but in order to make it work I must allow myself to own my own personal views and beliefs. I used to think it was selfish to put myself first, in fact, I've been told it is selfish for me to put myself before other people. 'Love your neighbor as yourself.' Why has it taken me so long to figure out that loving myself first is the key to finding my peace? I must put my beliefs first, then own them. Then I can give out with confidence what I've decided and know to be truth. This is love. This is peace."

I am no longer trying to control the environment around me, over which I have no power. I have come to accept that I'm not able to love others perfectly either. I don't know people well enough to know what they want or need. My husband has taught me this lesson many times. Robert shows me love by washing the car, mowing the lawn or whatever else needs to be done around the house. I, on the other hand, show him love by asking about his day, talking about his feelings and holding his hand on evening walks. The problem we have to work through is that he gives me what he views as loving and I do the same. Robert and I are constantly learning to show each other love by asking ourselves, *what can I do to make the other person feel loved?* A lot of times the answer is different from what I would do myself. I am learning to look outside myself and simply give without expecting in return.

20

WHAT'S LOVE GOT TO DO WITH IT?

When it comes to love, I am continually being taught lessons through life experiences. When I expect something back from the love I give out, I can really miss the blessing. The lessons I share in this chapter are the kind I would like to get all the time. They are the fun lessons of life!

I sold my balloon shop when I was pregnant with our son. After he was born, some friends I had recently come to know sent me a gift of love. When the doorbell rang, I saw the old familiar balloon truck in front of our house. The delivery boy handed me a balloon bouquet from all the members of this group. I looked fondly at all their signatures. They couldn't have known that I used to own this business and also designed this bouquet myself. I giggled as I wrote each thank you note leaving out this small minor detail.

A short while later, the tables were turned. I had a new friend who collected a particular group of items, so for Christmas I added to her collection, even getting it signed by the artist. I could tell she was impressed. So was I. I really did it right! The next Christmas came around so I decided to repeat the gift, right down to the artist's signature. She received my gift with excitement and love. I knew I had given her something really special. A few months later, I told another friend how much I enjoyed giving my gift to this person because I could tell she really appreciated it. To my surprise, I found out that this woman's husband owned the company that produced the gift!

I have pondered these two stories from time to time, thinking about how it relates to love. I designed my balloon arrangement for the purpose of making others feel loved and accepted. How exciting to receive it and experience it for myself!

I still have to ask myself, "Am I trying to earn people's approval with all my good works or am I doing good works out of love for them from my heart, in turn making them feel loved and accepted?"

In order to love and accept others, I also need to learn to forgive. Forgiveness is not about what somebody did to me or about what happened to me. It's not about outside forces doing me wrong. It is about forgiving others for not meeting my expectations.

Recently, when someone said something mean about me, I felt hurt. I called Joan to talk about this woman in not too complimentary terms. After I hung up, I realized that what I'd done was not necessary. I wanted to be validated at someone else's expense. What I said to Joan was not helpful to either of us. I obviously put expectations on this person to give me their approval or I wouldn't have been hurt when they didn't give it to me.

I have found many times that loving other people is a decision I need to make ahead of time. I plan my day when I wake up and look at my schedule. I know the kids have school and need to be there at a certain time so I plan accordingly. After school, I already know that my children have sports activities. When I pick them up at school, I have already prepared ahead of time to bring their clothes and gym equipment. I go down the street that will get me to their games and if I'm really on the ball, I have dinner in the crock-pot ready to eat when we get home that evening. All these things I do ahead of time because I have decided beforehand the consequences I want. Anytime I begin to plan something, it starts with the outcome I want to achieve.

Thanksgiving and Christmas are planned holidays on the calendar every year. Sometimes I make preparations months before the actual event so that the outcome I have in mind is accomplished. Why is it I don't do this more often when I make choices that hurt other people or myself? I say something ugly that doesn't need to be said and before I know it, someone has been hurt. I need to back up, remember the goal is love and make a different choice in what I say.

21

ACCEPTING WHAT CAN'T
BE CHANGED

I realize that what I have shared about my past is only my perspective and I'm sure other people have a different opinion.

Growing up with someone who is bipolar was extremely painful. It was also very difficult trying to relate to a mother whose thought patterns were so scattered that I couldn't grasp reason or find order. Nothing for me came easy and often times I was certain I was the odd one out. It wasn't until years later that I discovered I wasn't the crazy one.

A person living in chaos realizes at a very young age that relating to other people is almost impossible. I was always making people mad by the inappropriate things I would say or do.

Forgiving myself for my past, in turn, gave me my self-worth. Then I internalized and believed that I was worth a great deal so I extended myself grace (which of course was always available to me.) This freed me up to accept myself right where I was.

When a person learns to accept himself, other people's successes or failures don't threaten him and there is no need to feel or act defensive. People are freed up at this point to extend grace to other people because they are no longer judging others by what is in them to begin with.

There has been a lot of pain behind my past and I have had the option of not forgiving myself or of going forward by celebrating life.

I want to always keep my sense of humor because life is too short to complain about what can't be changed. Both my brother and sister have dealt with the past of our family in their own way. We have all made choices based on what we think is best for our own lives and I give them the freedom to make their own decisions. I have chosen to move on in a different direction than my family.

I'm thankful for what I went through growing up because my past is what formed me into becoming who I am today. I have been able to take these dysfunctional situations and turn them around to be used for good.

People have said that bad things can't be used for good. I disagree. I believe everything happens for a purpose. One of the keys of healing and finding peace in your life is not to fall into self-pity. It is also important to not give up on people. I have found that there are a lot of people who care about others and give out the love they have received. There are those who are willing to be my teacher and have never quit believing in me. I want to continue to strive towards grace as well.

I have found that I can look to my spiritual family and ask myself the same question Jesus asked, "'. . . Who is my mother, and who are my brothers?' Pointing to his disciples, he said, 'Here are my mother and my brothers. For whoever does the will of my Father in heaven is my brother and sister and mother.'" (Matthew 12:48–49) My spiritual family has become my true family. I am thankful for those people.

We are not promised an easy road ahead. Coming to a crossroads in my life and having to make a decision to face my chaos was the hardest thing I have ever done. I was brought to a place in my journey where I had to make some tough choices.

When my car is running near empty, I begin looking for a place to fill up. I could try to save money and time by filling it with the bottled water I have in my hand, but it won't work. There is only one thing I know of that will make my car run and that is gas. I don't like running out of gas because if I do, I have to walk several miles to find a filling station amongst lots of dangerous traffic. If I have my children with me, then it really becomes a problem because I have no other choice but to take them with me. Now, I've put them in danger and we're all on this road together. Instead of placing all these people in jeopardy, I have learned it makes my life a lot easier to stick with what works and fill up my tank on a regular basis.

I tried for years to fill my emotional tank with things it was not designed for. I was getting nowhere fast. My need for peace and the pain I was in became greater than my chaos I had accepted for so long. I chose to get out of the chaos!

22

CROSSING THE BRIDGE TO PEACE

I watched a segment on *Country Reporter* in which a man was dressed in a Santa suit traveling down the streets of an unnamed city. People were walking on the sidewalks wearing business apparel going wherever their schedules led them. Santa attracted a lot of attention. People of all ages would wave, shake his hand and introduce themselves without even thinking. Santa gripped the arms of men in their sixties and seventies, men with briefcases who had an agenda. These men forgot their pressures for a brief moment while they skipped down the streets with Santa, their childlike innocence peeking through their tough exteriors.

Funny how an ordinary person can dress up to depict a time when we all shared dreams, hopes and the innocence of childhood. What happens? What causes childlike faith to disappear? The once-forgiving child learns to protect himself with walls invisible to the human eye but very visible to a God who sees all. We begin to play games, incorporating our own agenda. Internalized hurt and pain take over as we learn to control other people, manipulating them through our words and actions.

Peace comes when I accept what cannot be changed. No matter what my dilemma, the ultimate goal is not to try and change the circumstances. What an unbelievable burden it would be if it were our job to come up with all the answers for our unresolved issues. The goal is in being honest with ourselves about who we are and what we've become, and then change from within.

Life's not always easy. I still have fears I need to overcome. I knew I needed to be honest about who I had become because it was much better than the alternative, which was pretending I was okay. Crossing the bridge from chaos to peace takes a lot of guts. It is scary at times and requires a person to make a lot of changes. This journey can be very uncomfortable but I can assure you that it is well worth the risks you will take.

Psalm 95:7–8 says, "Today, if you hear his voice, do not harden your hearts. . . ." Henri J.M. Nouwen says, "When we have met our Lord in the silent intimacy of our prayer, then we will also meet him . . . in the market and in the town square. But when we have not met him in the center of our own hearts, we cannot expect to meet him in the busyness of our daily lives." Or another source, an ancient Egyptian proverb says, "When hearing is good, speaking is good." May we learn to listen so that we may speak truth and grace.

To order additional copies of

Out
of

Chaos

A Journey Toward Peace

Have your credit card ready and call

Toll free: (877) 421-READ (7323)

or send $10.99* each, plus $3.95** S&H to

WinePress Publishing
PO Box 428
Enumclaw, WA 98022

www.winepresspub.com

*Washington residents please add 8.6% tax.
**Add $1.00 S&H for each additional book ordered